your

FACE

The Place of *Blessing*

The Place
of Relationship,
Intimacy
and Truth

by DeLoris jacqueline Moore

A Taste of Jesus Ministries
P.O. Box 396 • Flossmoor, IL 60422-0396
Email: atoj100@sbcglobal.net

First published by AuthorHouse 11/04/05

ISBN: 1-4208-8272-4 (sc)

Library of Congress Control Number: 2005907991

Printed in the United States of America
Mattoon, Illinois

Dedication

This book is dedicated to Rachel Angela, my daughter, whose face has been a "Place of Blessing" to me from the time she was born until now. This simple poem, best tells the story.

To My Rachel Angela,

What can I say, but "Thank you Lord,
For giving my Rachel to me?"

How can I ever repay you Lord?
Her love for you led me to thee.

Oh, how You've caused the fruit of my womb,
To help me press on through the nights.

No one but You knows the whole truth dear Lord,
She's helped me to climb higher heights.

Oh, the depth of Your love for her Lord,
I believe she knows you, better than I.

I ask You, Oh Lord, Almighty God,
Please grant her a "Shalom" life.

Yes, Rachel, my only, you have honored me so,
For you loved me before I was found.

My prayer for you now, Oh Sunshine of mine,
May He take you to higher ground.

So sing His praises and proclaim His Word,
Do not fear, and never give in.

For you were created to go forth and heal,
Rachel Angela, you, were created to win.

Acknowledgements

My thanks and gratitude to the following people, whose faces have imparted the blessings of love, mercy, grace, peace, acceptance, and encouragement. May the Lord look over His Word in Numbers 6:22-27, and perform it in your lives.

- Apostle George Aja, (Embassy Christian Center). My Apostolic Covering and Overseer, who prophetically commanded me to "Write the book."

- To Jim Herron, a businessman who came to my home and gave me a King James Bible in 1973, which I begin to read and be changed.

- Pastor Varnado, (Normal Park Baptist Church). The Pastor who continued to encourage me to come back to Church in 1974.

- Pastor Walter & Sue Pedersen, (Homewood Full Gospel Church). My Pastors, teachers and friends since 1978.

- Pastor George Thomas, (All Nations Community Church). My Pastor, teacher and advisor for 12 years.

- Apostle Jane Hansen, (Aglow International). Whose face has imparted to me love, acceptance, grace, wisdom and friendship. I have been honored to serve in Aglow since 1981 and under her direct leadership since 1996.

- To the Directors, Leaders and Advisors of A Taste of Jesus Ministries: Lois, Lynn, Martha, Rachel, Janet, Yvonne, Ellen, Geraldine, Ernestine, Mary Ann, Carmen, Isamae, Othea, Alice, Denise, Michelle, Kim, Marie, Jackie, Sarah, Joanne, Dorothy, Christine, Bernard Holland, Pastor Florence Shy and Pastors Otis and Thelma Leftwich, who continue to help me run with the Vision. May the Lord reward you greatly.

- To all our partners, volunteers and financial supporters. May the Lord reward you 30, 60 and 100 fold.

- To all of my sisters, relatives and extended family. I love you dearly.

- To the five-fold ministry vessels who have poured into my life.

- To all of my Aglow International sisters around the globe who have opened their doors, allowing me to "Go into all the world and preach the Gospel of Jesus Christ."

- Finally, to my best friends, Martha and Oliver Baylor, whom I know were sent into my life by the Lord in 1978 and who have held up my arms with prayer, love, support, encouragement and wise counsel. May we grow old together.

Table of Contents

Introduction

In October of 2002, I spoke at a National Conference in Portugal for Aglow International. The Conference theme was on Relationship. I was scheduled for three sessions.

In preparation for the Conference, I studied various aspects of relationship, such as, interpersonal relationships, surface type relationships, family, marriage, friendships, male/female and so on.

I noticed there is one common thread necessary in all relationships and that is "the face." This led me to meditate on the fact that "the face" is the one part of the body that is usually **not** covered. It is usually visible for all to see.

During my research, I believe I discovered a major reason why our faces were created to be seen by others. The answer may be found in many books, but one specific book is the Bible, in the Book of Numbers, Chapter 6, verses 22-27.

In summary, these six verses indicate that God gave a command to Moses to tell Aaron the High Priest and his sons, how they were to bless the Israelites, God's chosen people.

Moses was advised to tell them that the blessing was to be "spoken" over the people. This blessing is a powerful one, in that it speaks of the LORD blessing, keeping, watching and guarding His people. It speaks of the "Face" of the LORD, shining upon them, with grace (unmerited favor). It also speaks of the "Face" of the LORD being lifted up with approval and giving them peace through His countenance.

Last but not least, the LORD said to Moses, "So they (the priests) shall put (invoke) My name on the children of Israel, and I will bless them." This in itself is a powerful revelation. First, it reveals to us what the LORD considers a blessing. Second, it reveals to us that when we bless someone in the name of the LORD, that it is the same as placing or invoking His name upon that person. The LORD then goes on to say that when He sees His name invoked upon that person, He will bless them.

Meditating on these scriptures more and more caused me to realize that God had many purposes for making us in His image and likeness. He had a specific purpose in mind when He made our faces. His purpose I believe was that we would be willing to do with our face, what He does with His. He desired that we would be willing for our face to become "A Place of Blessing." A place where others could receive a blessing instead of a curse.

Hopefully as you read the various chapters and topics, you too will discover what an awesome part of your body your face is and was created to be.

Hopefully you will quickly be able to identify yourself and others as you realize that "the face" is the place where all true relationship begins. It is the place where you are either accepted or rejected, esteemed or mocked, loved or hated, exalted or humiliated. It is a place of great power, this face of yours. Its members (eyes, ears, nose and mouth) hold the keys to life and death.

Hopefully you will be enlightened, and even healed of the deep wounds caused by negative words, blatant rejection, humiliation, fiery darts and other things that have been imparted to you through the face(s) of others.

Most things are first natural, then spiritual. Therefore the first half of this book speaks of the purpose and power of your face, from a natural perspective. The second half of this book reveals the purpose and power of your face from a spiritual perspective.

Finally, it is my hope that you will choose to allow "your face" to become a "place of blessing" for others and in turn, allow yourself to receive a blessing from the faces of others, even from those you do not even know.

Chapter One:

<u>That's Not Nice Little Girl</u>

> ". . . be not afraid of their faces: for I am with thee
> to deliver thee (Jeremiah 1:8)."

<u>That's Not Nice Little Girl</u>

"That's not nice little girl," said my great grandfather who was 90 years plus, as he sat at the kitchen table directly across from me. His wrinkled, scraggily face had such a harsh look of disapproval. It frightened me so much that I almost wet my panties.

Big crocodile tears began to form in my eyes and spill down my cheeks. I thought to myself, "What had I said that "wasn't nice?" I had only responded to my grandmother's second request to eat some "boiled" carrots she had made for dinner. When the carrots were passed to me the first time, I hurriedly passed them down the table without taking any for myself.

My grandmother graciously said to me, "Dee Dee Hall, don't you want some of those good carrots?" "No, Mama, I said. I don't like boiled carrots." Grandma, or Mama as I called her, continued to try and convince me to eat some boiled carrots.

She said, "Carrots are so good for your eyes and they will even make you pretty."

I responded to her reply in a tiny small voice, "I don't care," at which time my great grandfather gave me "the look" and said to me in no uncertain terms, with a voice that shook my very insides, "That's not nice, little girl!"

To the best of my memory, my great-grandfather's face was the first face that imparted great fear and dis-approval to me. I was not only afraid that I was going to get a "whippin," but I was thoroughly confused as to what I had said or done "that was not nice." I really did not know that when you told the truth about something, if you happened to be a small child, it was considered as "sassing" or "talking back" and of course "that's not nice."

I recall sniffling my nose as the hot tears ran down my face. I reluctantly put some of the boiled carrots on my plate and even ate some. "Ugh!"

Great Grandpa's face was hardly the place of blessing to this four year-old little girl. This was the first time I recall feeling fear, shame, disapproval and rejection. I did not know the names of these feelings, but I know them now.

During wartime in the 40's I stayed at grandmother's house. I had three older sisters and a brand new baby sister. My mother worked in the war plant and I was not yet in school like my other sisters, so she took me to grandmother's house and I stayed there during the week until I was seven years old.

Grandfather had 14 living children. Six were by his first wife, who died shortly after giving birth to her seventh child, who also died. He married again four years later to the woman that I knew as Grandmother, and she gave him eight more children. The last two children grandma had were twin girls who were only three years older than me. We came up more like sisters than aunt and niece. In fact, I never called them Aunt until I was much older.

The Face of True Kinship

My mother was the oldest and her new mother was only 12 years older than she was. In those days, no one said "stepmother," at least not in my grandfather's house. I never knew my grandmother was not my mother's real mother until I was sixteen years old and my grandmother died. I was hurt when they told me, because I did not see why it made any difference. It was as though they were trying to take my "real" grandmother from me. My response was "I don't care, she is my real grandmother, because she was my only grandmother and she loved me and took care of me!" I refused to place her in any other place in my heart. I cried for many days after that. It was then, at age 16 that I adopted my own philosophy about certain things, namely, kinship.

My attitude became and still is this: A sperm does not a Father make and a womb does not a Mother make. It is the one who has loved, provided, protected, laughed, cried, taught, counseled, encouraged, punished, steered and reared you that is your Father, Mother, Grandfather, Grandmother etc.

My feelings toward kinship are that the actions must live up to the title. I still feel this way even though I understand family trees and that an adopted child may want to know his or her background. I sometimes get upset when the so- called "real" Father or Mother is located after the person is grown and the adopted child seems to quickly forget reality and kick the parents who truly became the "real" parents, to the curb. I am all for birth lineage, inheritance, family trees and such, but not at the expense of others who truly have made a great sacrifice in parenting someone else's children in the time of true need.

The Face of a Real Grandmother

Talk about a face that was a place of blessing; it was my grandmother. Her smile and deep chuckle made you feel approved of, loved, secure, and protected. Her face was one of great wisdom and her dark skin shined like olive oil. Her eyes could look right through you and you had to tell the truth.

Her hands were strong enough to wring out sheets over the tub until they were almost dry and yet gentle enough to give you a "camphorated oil rub down" if you were sick with a cold. How good her hands felt to my feet when I was five or six years old and had a bad cold. She would rub my feet and chest with salve and oil and then wrap me in a blanket and put my feet against a warm potbelly stove. Then she would look at me and smile and say 'feel better now?" How her face imparted love to me. I believe I got better because of her face.

Oh how I loved to be sick at Grandma's house. You got to sleep late, even as late as 10:00 in the morning, just in time for your favorite radio program, "Let's Pretend." Then you were called to wash up for breakfast and yours was always special because after all, you were not feeling well.

My special "sick" breakfast would always be a boiled egg, half grapefruit, toast and jelly and bacon or thick sausage link. There would also be milk, juice, potatoes and even biscuits if you could eat more. Yes, so much was imparted and instilled in me because of my grandmother's face. It was truly a place of blessing and still is because I have hidden her face in my heart.

I was named after my mother's younger sister who was born on the same day as my mom, January 23rd. Everyone called us both by the same nickname, "Dee Dee." Whenever anyone would call "Dee Dee," I would always come running. It was decided from that point on, to call me "Dee Dee Hall," so I would know when someone was really calling for me and not my Aunt Dee Dee.

The nickname "Dee Dee" as well as "Aunt Dee Dee" has followed me throughout my life. I do not have to even tell anyone. People just seem to automatically call me Aunt Dee Dee. I now have many spiritual nieces all over the world that have adopted me as their "Aunt Dee Dee." I believe this is because I have learned how to bless others with my face.

The Face of a Grand PaPa

My grandfather was a very large man, 300 pounds plus. He often sat on the back porch after work or in the living room reading the papers. He was usually quiet unless he was wearing his "discipline" hat.

One of my twin aunts was his favorite (at least that's what everyone said). He always called her name whenever he wanted something. "Shirley," he would call out in a loud voice sounding almost like Santa Claus, "Bring me some water!" Shirley would stop whatever she was doing and run to the kitchen to get Pa Pa some ice-cold water in the biggest Mason Jar she could find.

Grandma did a lot of fruit and vegetable canning and Grandpa liked to drink out of the glass jars. Secretly I wished he would call on me to get his water. Sometimes I would go up to him and ask if "I" could get his water.

One time I asked him and he said, "Yes." I was so delighted that I could get the water too. I remember so vividly how he looked at me, chuckled and gave me a smile and said, "That's so nice little girl," and then he gave me a big hug.

I guess back then, "little girl" was the politically correct name to call someone who was in fact a little girl.

When Grand Papa gave me his smile of approval, his face was a place of blessing to this seven year old "little girl," not to mention his hug. What a sense of approval, love and security!

This strong, loving and wise Grand Papa's face was usually a place of blessing to everyone. However, I recall a time when he became very angry with one of his children, because she had upset Grandma. (Whoever caused grandmother any problem did so at their own risk.)

One day, Grandma and my Aunt Patricia who was about 16 years-old, were having a verbal argument. It became heated and Grandma hit Aunt Pat. Aunt Pat raised her hand to hit Grandma back and she said, "Oh you're going to hit me back are you?"

Well Grand Papa was sitting in the living room and heard the commotion. He responded by calmly picking up the small "potbelly stove" shovel and calling Aunt Pat to come into the living room.

Pat walking and crying very slowly from the kitchen, knowing that her life just might be in jeopardy began to cry out, "Daddy I'm sorry, Daddy I'm sorry." Grand Papa paid no attention to her cries whatsoever, but said to her, "Oh, so you're going to hit your Mother are you? Oh, so you're going to hit my wife are you?" Then he said, "Hold out your hands" and when she did, he hit them with the shovel from the potbelly stove. Whack, whack, whack!

Aunt Pat screamed bloody murder and drew her hands back saying, "Daddy please don't hit me again, I'm sorry Daddy, I won't ever do it again." "Oh, you just might" Grand Papa said, "Hold out your hands!" Aunt Pat then fell to her knees as he hit her hands with the shovel again. Whack, whack!

I witnessed my aunt crawl on her knees backwards until she ended up in the kitchen where Grandma was and she cried, "Mama I am so sorry, please tell Daddy not to hit me again." Grandma then said "John, John, don't hit her anymore," at which time he turned, went back into the living room and sat down, leaving Aunt Pat to think about her big mistake.

To my knowledge Aunt Pat never ever raised her hand or even talked back to Grandma again. She had not encountered "the face of blessing" from her father, but instead "the face of wrath." I am sure she never forgot this incident as long as she lived.

Images of Unpleasant Faces

More often than not, the situations or circumstances we tend to remember are those where we have had an unpleasant "face-to-face" experience with someone. These are the images that are recorded deep in our mind and heart and tend to haunt us later on. The faces that God originally intended to be a blessing to us have often done the exact opposite.

A person's self esteem is often negatively impacted because someone's face (eyes, words, tenor and expression) has imparted fear, anger, disapproval,

7

shame, disgust, cursing, disdain, and/or mockery to them, instead of the "blessing" God intended for our faces to impart to others.

Unpleasant face-to-face encounters play a large role in how we see ourselves with regard to our ability to step into and fulfill our God given destiny. Many times, the impact of a negative face-to-face encounter is hidden so deeply, that it may be years before a person even recognizes the emotional damage that has been done. Inner wounding because someone's face imparted everything BUT the blessing. Inner wounding because someone has sent a negative message through their face. Inner wounding because someone's face has closed the door to the blessings of relationship, intimacy and truth.

However, consider the "Aaronic" blessing in the book of Numbers 6:24-27. It includes being kept and guarded; having the face of God shine upon you and be gracious and merciful to you, and having the Lord lift your spirit up with His face of approval. This **spoken** blessing includes receiving the peace of God that passes knowledge. It causes the recipient's heart and mind to be guarded from fear and instead, kept by the love, mercy, grace and peace of the Lord.

Once you become aware that this spiritual blessing that speaks of the face of God is for all who believe in Him, you can receive the blessing for yourself and then speak the same blessing of love, mercy, grace and peace to others.

Questions/Reflections:

1. Do you recall the first time you were the object of an unpleasant face?

2. Whose face was it?

3. What was the situation or circumstance?

4. Are you willing to forgive those who offended you?

5. If not, what is still causing you pain?

6. Have you addressed the issue(s) face-to-face with your offender?

7. What steps of reconciliation and restoration are you willing to take to bring about your healing?

Chapter Two:

Please Don't Laugh At Me

The Face of Mockery

When someone laughs with you, it is quite different than someone laughing at you. The physical, mental and emotional response to being laughed at by others, can cause what I like to call a paralysis and imprisoning of your abilities and dreams. The human response to being laughed at can and does cause negative energy to be released within your being. Negative energy (thoughts, feelings, decisions), can only produce negative actions and deeds.

In order to become a "place of blessing" in the lives of others, we must become aware of the "spirit of mockery", what it's motives are, and how it thinks and operates. Then we must examine ourselves, motives and actions and discover if we have been a "victim" of mockery and how it may have hindered our progress.

We must also be willing, if we ourselves have mocked others, to acknowledge it and change ourselves. Mockery comes through people and causes fear of failure, which in turn causes the desire to be perfect so no one will laugh at you.

One thing leads to another and before long you are a basket case of fear. My hope is as you go through this chapter, you will receive revelation, healing and deliverance along with the joy that comes from knowing the truth.

The Bible states that fear is a spirit. It also says God has not given us the spirit of fear, but a spirit of power, love and a sound mind (II Tim 1:7). Let me just say to you, "Make no mistake about it, *mockery is a spirit that works through people!"*

Mockery is one of the most treacherous spirits operating in the world today. It will hinder you, imprison your talents, abilities and creativity. Mockery will keep you from becoming all that you were born and destined to be.

It is a spirit whose sole purpose is to rob, kill and destroy YOU. Its ultimate objective is to humiliate you in public or in the intimate presence of others. It is one of the most ugly spirits that the enemy of our souls desires to fill people with, including people who profess to know God.

Mockery is a deceiving spirit most times, as it often manifests itself as a friend, an angel of light if you will. It tries to mask itself with a smile. The spirit of mockery usually ends up revealing itself, because it is often full of pride, envy and/or jealousy. It exposes itself by its supposedly innocent words and expressions.

A smile, a chuckle, a laugh, a wink, a joke, with you being the butte end of it, is usually the modus operandi for the spirit of mockery.

Mockery is all about laughing at you, pointing fingers at and belittling you. A person being used by the spirit of mockery often tries to appear very innocent by accompanying their questions and snide remarks with a seemingly innocent smile, smirk or chuckle.

People controlled by mockery seek to embarrass others and are quick to feign innocence if challenged. "Oh I didn't mean anything by what I said, I was just asking," or "I was just making a statement," or "I was just playing or joking, don't be so touchy!" or "You are just too sensitive."

Again, it has a bulls eye objective, which is:

1) To fill you with fear of the "faces" of mockery;

2) To keep you from believing in your ability to progress and move forward; and

3) To cause you to doubt that you could be successful in reaching your highest potential and fulfilling the destiny God has planned for your life.

I have discovered that people, including you and I that desire to mock others, somewhere along the line are not pleased with themselves. Mocking others often helps them to cover up the serious issues of their hearts and minds.

Focusing on the imperfections of others keeps the mockers from having to deal with their own garbage. Laughing at the efforts of others covers up the fact that most times they do not have the courage themselves to put forth the same effort and step out on the limb of "trying, attempting, discovering and achieving."

The sad thing is the person who allows the spirit of mockery to operate in them and control them, will never achieve their hearts desire or fulfill their wildest dreams. Why? Because they themselves are fearful and insecure and mocking others only serves to increase their own insecurity and fear of failure.

You must decide not to become a victim of the faces of mockery. Being afraid of "their" faces, will keep you from discovering the ability within you and giving "such as you have" to others. Fearing the faces of others closes the door to true relationships, since the face is meant to be the place where relationship begins. Again, it is the place of giving and receiving.

If we would think of the face as the very earth from which it came, then we would conclude that what we sow into the face (earth) will be the harvest that we reap. The seeds we sow with our face will come back in our face sooner or later. If we really understood this, we would make sure we use our face to sow good seeds, so we will reap a good harvest ourselves.

The Face of Perfection vs. Excellence

The spirit of perfection is different from the spirit of excellence. Excellence accomplishes success based on faith and confidence coupled with the joy of achievement.

Fear of mockery opens the door to the face and spirit of perfection that is different than the spirit of excellence. The perfectionist does achieve success, but usually has confidence only in what it already knows; tends not to pursue ambiguous areas and when it does, the fear of failure or mockery often causes creative and explorative abilities to become locked up.

Perfectionists tend to expect more of themselves than they ought. They tend to expect success the first time around. They often expect success without seeking additional knowledge, because they have been able to succeed without much studying. They are usually "A" students or at a minimum "B+" and more often

13

than not, have achieved their status without much effort. Not that they do not work hard at what they do, but what they do is not always "effort" for them. Much of what others do that requires major effort, the perfectionist can do with their eyes closed.

Perfectionists usually do not like or expect to do anything over again or more than once. Major effort, checking and rechecking is spent on "doing it right the first time and only doing it once." Perfectionists are not accustomed to many corrections because of the effort they put into their work the first time around.

Again, perfectionists don't like doing things over and over and as a result, tend to limit their achievements. They often interpret doing something over as failure and are afraid or anxious about what others might say when they hear about their failure or lack of success.

Perfectionists sometimes even go through physiological changes when their educational test papers are corrected. How do I know? Because I discovered a few years ago, that I have been a prisoner of the spirit of perfection and was never aware of it.

Two Major Traits of a Perfectionist

I always thought a perfectionist was simply an immaculate, neat, organized person, with a place for everything and everything in its place. One who was obsessed with cleanliness and neatness. I never equated myself with being a perfectionist because although I like things clean and neat, I have always had so many things to do, I have had to let some things go. In fact in some areas, I am somewhat junky because I do not have time for filing papers, purging files, purging closets etc.

I would be the last one to even think I was a perfectionist in any way. I must admit that certain things I like done with taste, like setting a table. I also like things to be balanced. (A throw rug on the floor must be placed evenly between the couch and tables, but this is not really a perfectionist is it?)

However at an annual business meeting a few years ago, I found out that I had at least two major traits of a perfectionist:

1) ***Perfectionists don't like to do anything twice.*** The thought of it used to make me upset, and angry. I felt as though I didn't pass my test. I just did not want to put forth "all" that effort over again, just to correct a simple error like a typo or misspelled word, or redo an entire arithmetic paper just to insert a step that was missed. I just went bonkers.

   Hitting the bull's eye the first time around was my objective. I did not like repeats, or re-runs. This came from the fact that in school, I often received 90's and 100's on my tests the first time around. I was not accustomed to doing anything more than once. I did not and still do not care to do the same thing over and over again. I like NEW, new development, new furniture, new clothes, new ideas, and new achievements, new, new, new!

   I now believe that this is what has kept me from pursuing my full destiny, all these years, including writing books, because I dreaded having to write, and rewrite, write and rewrite which I now realize I equated with failure. Books have been inside of me over 10 years but I believe the thought of rejection played a huge role in the paralysis because I was not accustomed to failure.

2) ___Perfectionists often equate criticism with failure.___

When I was in elementary school in the early grades, I used to feel as though I was naked and had done something wrong when I got my paper back from the teacher all marked up in red pen.

I did not realize that at this young age, because I was accustomed to achieving 100% on almost every paper, I then equated a wrong answer or criticism with failure. This also meant to me, that I had failed "to please" my teacher.

I never understood why the teacher had to mark up my entire paper with a big red check mark or write her comments in red ink. It felt like she was deliberately destroying my work, which was a representation of who I was. Those red marks were like stab marks to my soul. I not only felt like I was being cut up, but it felt like the teacher may have enjoyed doing it. Was she angry with me? Was she disappointed in me? Was she laughing at my wrong answers? What had I done but try to understand everything she said?

Couldn't she have written her comments over to the side and in another color? Did she have to draw "X's" and scribble her comments over my entire paper? (During that time, I was not able to identify what I really felt, all I knew is that I felt like I had failed and been rejected, even though my score was still very good.) I even received three double promotions, skipping three elementary grades, but I still could not deal with those corrections done in red and for years, I never really knew why. I did not know it was the fear of failure.

A Child's Fear of Failure and Mockery

Now as a young child, I probably felt like this, because I always got very good grades, even though I did not always feel confident. Others said I was very smart because I graduated at twelve years of age from elementary school.

I was always afraid that one day, my grades would not be good and then "they" would find out that I was not as smart as everyone had thought all those years.

Graduating elementary school at age twelve caused great fear to enter my life. I realize now, it came from the fear of failure and the fear of being humiliated by the laughter and mocking of others. Although I graduated from high school at age 16, I still remember being terrified to apply for college because I had to write an essay and I feared it would not be good enough for college acceptance.

Would you believe that I was even afraid I might not be able to find my class room, making me late which meant the whole class would laugh at me behind my back or in my face, because I was too stupid to find my class. Needless to say I was 30 years old before I finally went to college. By then I was married, had a daughter, worked full time and only took up two years of computer science, but never obtained a college degree.

False/Self Confidence

Now figure this out. In spite of this spirit of perfection that was operating big time in me, I was very successful in whatever I had confidence that I "could" do. I always loved to learn and loved to take tests. There was something about taking a test that gave me a sense of achievement because I always passed it. Yet the fear of failure that began as a teenager plagued me throughout the years, keeping me from utilizing my ability to full capacity. I always played it safe in school and never took educational courses that others had failed or told me were too hard to pass. I determined never to put myself in a position where I could possibly fail. I then began to try and control the outcome of every area of my life.

The fear of failure has an imaginary "voice" which often comes through people. Though I had confidence in some areas, if someone older than me had already failed at something, I steered clear of attempting success in that area. The imaginary "voice" of the fear of failure was not only about what my mother and sisters would say, but it was more about what my aunts and the family next door would say.

This voice of the fear of failure used to say to me, "What will the Smith's say?" or "What will the Williams say?" if they ever found out that you failed a class or had a car accident or became pregnant or could not get a good job. Whatever will they say and how will you ever save face?"

I recall as a teenager, being an avid reader of "funny book" or "comic book" and so-called "true love" magazine stories. I use to pretend that like so many of the stories, I would take a train to another city and make good. Then I would see myself coming back to the old neighborhood, very successful, and finally getting approval and not mockery from the two families that I feared the most.

Why did I fear the Smith's? Because they were always mocking and laughing at other people; Always talking and belittling others. Always putting others down; calling them silly names and criticizing and passing judgment on everyone that passed by their house.

I was always afraid that when I went home, I too would be the object of their mockery. My physiological reaction when I thought about it was the same as the teacher marking my papers with red ink. I so wanted their approval because I did not like what I felt when they laughed at other people.

Please understand that these were adult neighbors and I was only 10-15 years old. The Smith's became the "they" in my life. They became the foundation for being afraid of the faces of other people and being afraid of being judged by others. I do not recall them ever saying anything positive or complimentary about anyone. Maybe they did, but that is not what I remember. Yet I truly loved them and inwardly hungered for their approval and acceptance.

I stayed over their house all the time even though their favorite phrase concerning me was "Dee Dee Hall, you're a big fool." They would say this whenever I would be sitting with them and suddenly start humming or singing softly. They would then say, "You've got company in case you didn't know it. Girl, what's on your mind…what are you thinking about? You're a big fool Dee Dee Hall! Ha, ha, ha. Next you will be answering yourself. Ha, ha, ha. Big fool!"

Later on, I began to say things about myself just to make them laugh. When they were laughing about what I said about myself, it made me feel better. At least I talked about my own self rather than being afraid they would talk about me after I went home. I learned early in life how to "play the fool" to keep from feeling like I was a fool. I learned to make people laugh to keep from feeling mocked. I learned to become a clown because it was a sure way of being "liked" by everyone. Fifty years later this family has not yet discovered God's purpose for their faces.

Why did I fear the Williams? They represented the family clan with all its real and imagined expectations. I came from "good stock" that appeared to succeed at everything. There was so much pride in our family name. The thought of certain relatives in my family knowing that I had failed at anything was almost unbearable to me as a young person. After all, I was a "Williams."

Looking back, it was all a myth, as many in our so-called "good stock" family did not come anywhere near reaching their full potential. Some were successful (mostly the women), while others wasted their knowledge through pride and arrogance, and a "know-it-all spirit," resulting in failure and defeat.

The Know-it-all Spirit

Another spirit that tends to be associated with the spirit of perfection is that of a "know-it-all." Webster's Dictionary defines a know-it-all as "one claiming to know everything." There have been times that others have called me a know-it-all. This has been a puzzle to me, because I am the first to admit that I do NOT know it all. However, what I "think" I know, I really think I know which probably gives others the perception that I think I know everything.

I believe I have a virtue to a fault and that is my desire to share, tell, train and explain everything I do know with others. I believe that others may have been offended when I have shared things that I was excited about knowing, as they may have felt that I evidently thought they did not know it either.

Often others can misread our hearts and motives which causes us to be puzzled by their response to what we thought was a good thing. Once I asked the Lord; "If I truly have a know-it-all spirit, will you point it out to me, explain it to me and help me lay it down so I would not continue to offend others?"

A few years ago, I believe the Lord helped me define a person that has a know-it-all spirit. His definition was not one of condemnation, but rather revelation:

Yes, there are those, that think they know it all and it is difficult for others to tell them anything. Yes, there are those, that are not easy to be entreated. Then there are those, that mean no harm, but are often mis-understood.

Basically, a "know-it-all spirit" is simply a person that truly believes that they have obtained or received enough information/data for them to make a wise choice and decision. Therefore, they believe they do not need to read, research, wait or discuss the matter any further, because they think they **already know** all they need to know to move ahead.

Again, the person who is a perfectionist has a tendency to become a "know-it-all" and does not have to do a lot or studying or put forth a lot of effort to achieve what the average person achieves. This asset, often turns into a liability as they often seek only a minimum amount of information on any given subject/project. Again, they actually believe they have studied, or obtained enough information to make a wise final decision.

Watch out, if your mindset says, "I do not **have** to read the entire book. I will read the beginning, middle and end and then I will have enough knowledge and wisdom to make whatever decisions I need to make."

Watch out, if you tend to listen to the failures of others and base your decisions on that limited information, believing that "This is all I need to know about this issue." Make sure your decisions are based on "studying and understanding the matter," rather than "I know all I need to know."

Looking back over my life, I have made some decisions that I thought were wise based on what I thought "I knew," only to discover years later, that I had been driven by a know-it-all spirit which made me think that I "had enough information on the subject" to make a wise decision. Thank God for His continuous "On the journey training."

A good example was the time I "thought" I had received enough information to make a decision NOT to buy income property. I had always wanted to buy a 4 or 6 flat building as a younger person. I had obtained a job that would have allowed me to make such an investment. However, I began to gather information, most of it from people I worked with, who already had buildings. I listened to their complaints and in error considered it complete knowledge. They complained about the issues with regard to maintaining the building, renting the apartments and ongoing tenant problems. The complaints included calls in the middle of the night, having to get up at 2:00AM and travel to the City to unstop toilets etc.

So my "know-it-all spirit" truly believed it had received enough information to make a wise decision, which was NOT to purchase investment properties.

I did not put forth the effort to study, ponder and consider further before making my final decision. I did not stop to think, that complaints are not necessarily knowledge. I did not stop to think that my co-workers who kept saying how hard it was, were no longer cashing their employment checks, but just putting them in the bank. I did not stop to consider that they kept on purchasing more and more rental properties.

I did not study the tax breaks, even if there had been no cash flow because of maintenance costs. I did not consider having property where someone else paid my house note. No, instead, I knew that I knew I was not able to handle rental property because of the complaints and in my perception, failures of others.

Again, it has only been the past 7 years that I have discovered and understood how this awful spirit of mockery and perfection had paralyzed the creative ability in me. But thanks be unto God who gives us the victory and causes us to know and understand the truth, and the truth enlightens us and makes us free.

The Invisible Faces Named "They"

The faces of "They" have been one of the most fearful faces one could ever imagine. These faces named "They" are ones that we have not seen, but yet they have taken control of our imagination. The faces of "They" have crippled us, given us dreams of goblins and demons and filled us with terror, fear, dread, anxiety and every other synonym for fear.

The imaginary faces of "They" should not control or drive our decision-making process or become our criteria for planning our future.

How often have
<u>your decisions been based on:</u>

What will "They" say? What if "They" don't like this? What if "They" find out? Suppose "They" laugh at me? What will "They" think of me? I don't know how "They" might feel.

My question to you is this: Who **on earth is "They"?**

I have come to the conclusion that even though "They" can represent faces that you actually know, more often than not, "They" are those **invisible imaginary faces** that you fear will mock, reject and curse you instead of accepting, blessing and relating to you.

Who are "They?" The imaginary boogey man in the closet?

"They" are our invisible audience. "They" are those that would laugh at us, throw tomatoes and potatoes at us, even yell at us "Get off the stage!"

Who are "They?" Those that would talk about us behind our back; Those that would judge and even condemn our choices; decision, dreams and visions as idiotic, stupid, nonsense, useless and such like.

Who are "They?" Those faces that you may have met and have no desire to meet again. Those faces that you have witnessed others receive negative comments and everything but a blessing from. **These then, are "They."**

Fear of "Their" Faces

I remember how I felt as a seventh grade student at school during weekly assembly hall gatherings. Often when someone would sing a song and suddenly go off key, the laughter and mocking of the kids was awful. I could actually feel the embarrassment of the person singing. I recall vowing that I would never put myself in a position for others to laugh at my attempts.

This fear spilled over into my life for years. I always desired to sing in the church choir or with a singing group when I was a teen-ager, and was even told I had a good voice. However, I was afraid of auditioning because of the fear of mockery, so I never got to sing in the choir. Fifty years later, who is singing all over the place? You guessed it. There is nothing like being set "free to be."

Fear's purpose is always to keep you from stepping out of your area of confidence or your comfort zone, and stepping into God's area of limitless possibilities.

7 Steps in Overcoming the Spirit and Fear of Mockery

Once you understand the objectives of the spirit of mockery, you become a candidate to overcome. When the eyes of your understanding are enlightened, you begin to "see" your way. Seeing your way means you will understand:

1) The divisive schemes of the enemy of your soul;

2) Others are only able to give to you what they have "in" them, regardless of what you desire or need "from" them;

Let your face impart to others what you desire to receive from their face. If you desire approval, then give approval first. If you desire a smile, then you smile first. If you want a compliment, then you give one first. If you desire to be heard, then be willing to listen to others first.

Be willing to give to the faces of others what you want to receive from their faces. Love? Then give love first. Respect? Then give respect first. We often tend to demand from others what we should have first given to them.

3) Do not expect or demand from others what only God can give to you;

4) You must be willing to forgive others for not being as loving, merciful, understanding and kind to you as God Himself is willing to be.

5) God did not create or give to you a spirit of fear, timidity or dread.

6) You do not have to "receive from or believe in" any face that is not imparting to you a blessing and/or a promise of an open and honest, safe and healthy respectful and loving relationship.

7) You should sincerely hope and pray that the people, whose faces have imparted negative messages to you, would be freed from their unresolved issues. Abuse, rejection, envy, jealousy, unforgiveness, anger, resentment, bitterness, sorrow, pain and such, all play a role in someone's face sending negative messages because the person is simply sending or manifesting what is on the inside of them. ***Others cannot give what they do not have within***.

Questions/Reflections

1. Have you ever been the object of mockery?

2. What was it concerning?

3. How did it hinder your progress?

4. How do you plan to overcome the fear of others laughing or talking about you?

5. Can you identify with the spirit of perfection? If so, in what way(s)?

6. What is your strategy to overcome this trait?

7. Identify the faces named "They" that have impacted your decisions, vision and life.

8. What have you learned in this chapter that will positively affect your life?

Chapter Three:

Martha's Daughters

A Mother's Image

Whenever my relatives see me, they say "you are the spitting image of your mother." One of my sisters greets me with "Hi Mama" whenever she sees me.

My mother's name was Martha and her face was similar to my grandfather's. It could be the place of blessing or the place of sorrow if she was at her wits' end. She had what I call one of the most friendly, warm, inclusive, loving, kind, non-intimidating, non-criticizing and understanding faces I have ever known.

Please, do not misunderstand, like her father, my mother's face was the place of blessing "most" of the time. She expected obedience and it was something about her that made you want to please her. To hear Mama say "that's good," "you are smart," "the house looks nice," "you ironed my uniform real good this time," was like receiving a prize.

The best time to observe and receive the blessing from my mother's face was while she was cooking. Oh how her face shined. This was the time to ask for favors, while her countenance was glowing and she was singing. "Ma, can I have a nickel?" while she was whipping up the mashed potatoes or the cake. She would say as she tasted the potatoes, "Umm, look on the cocktail table. Hurry back now." Or "Ma, can I go outside to play?" (although my bed was not yet made). For a little while she'd say, "Don't forget you still have to make your bed." Then she'd look at you with that shining face and give you her blessing by smiling and letting you know she was aware of your manipulative tactics, but that it was still OK because she loved you so. Oh how she loved to cook and serve her family and others. Her reward was watching us eat her food and ask for more. Her food was so good, it made your nose run. Our table at breakfast or dinner was one to behold. Why there was humming and patting of the feet; moaning and sighing saying "Ooh Mama, you put your foot in this food."

Her "pocket book" and "clover leaf" style baked rolls melted in your mouth and could bring tears to you eyes, not to speak of her meat loaf, collard greens, string beans, candied sweet potatoes and boston baked beans with salt pork.

Her fried chicken recipe is still used by one of the biggest soul food restaurants in Chicago, Illinois, where she worked as the head cook. What can I say about her pork chops, fish, macaroni and cheese and pastries?

For breakfast there was bacon and sausage or ham along with the best-fried potatoes and onions. There were biscuits or pancakes, waffles or french toast.

Mama always told me that the food you cook would always reflect your attitude, and your emotions. She would chuckle and say, "When you burn your food, it's because you are thinking about a man."

She would say that you can taste food and tell if any "love" was stirred into the ingredients. Yes, it was a blessing indeed to see her face when she was

29

cooking. Later as she watched those who ate her food enjoy it so much, It was as though her face said, "for this cause, I was born." It was as though her heart was saying, "my purpose in life is to feed others; to fill them with comfort and joy; to give them strength for the journey; to change the countenance on their faces." Yes, I was born to "bless" and not "curse." Her face had a voice.

If you were smart, you tried to stay under the "blessing" umbrella. Mama was not really a hard taskmaster, but she ended up being a single parent, when she lost her only son at three years old. I was only one month old and there were three older girls, eight, seven and five years old.

My Father grieved over the loss of his only son and ended up having a nervous break down and was hospitalized for many years. Thus Ma became a single parent. Back in those days, it was even harder than it is now to raise children by yourself, because there were not as many family programs available.

Mama would divide up the chores among us and demand that we complete them. Not doing it caused you to have to look in her face, which was **not** the place of blessing when you had not polished the furniture, made up the beds, swept the living and dining room rugs, scrubbed the kitchen floor, cleaned the bath room or washed the dishes.

Her face was **not** the place of blessing when she would allow you go to bed and then wake you in the middle of the night to get up and complete the chores you did not finish. Her face was "the place of judgment." No matter how righteous the judgment, you did not feel blessed by her face as she said at two or three o'clock in the morning "DeLoris (notice not Dee Dee), get up and wash the dishes." You knew better than to respond with "but Ma, I'm sleepy."

You just knew better as you looked into that face of hers.

The Face of a New *White* Baby

Years went by and when my oldest sister was 15, Ma had another baby girl. I was seven years old then and Ma brought me home from living at my grandmother's because my sisters were old enough to watch me and see that I got to school. This new baby, became my "precious" baby sister.

My mother's face was one of great wisdom and often brought joy and laughter to us as she answered our many questions.

Many people do not understand that in an African/American family, the children can be various skin colors due to the mixture of blood from the days of slavery. Many people of color have blood mixed with Native American, European, West Indian or Asian. You name it and we probably have it.

This results in the children in one family being from light to dark pigmentation based on the mother and father and their true biological heritage.

When my baby sister was born, I was only seven years old. Back then you were told that the Stork brought the babies and that God made the babies.

She was very light and fair skinned silky black curly hair. She was the most beautiful baby I had ever seen. Her face was like that of a doll baby. Her head was tiny and round and her cheeks were red like rouge. Her lips were so tiny and thin and her eyes were black with blue around them. I could not believe she was my baby sister. I was afraid to touch her because she was so precious like breakable china. Oh how I loved my baby sister!

When she was only a few days old, my mother was reading the tag on her leg that had the statistics. She read her name, weight, length and date of birth. I then heard her say "colored," which was what we were called back then.

When I heard her say "colored" I jumped up and started clapping my hands and singing a song "she's colored, she's colored, my baby sister's colored, la, la, la, la, la, la, la, my baby sister's colored."

To that my mother laughed and laughed and said to me, "Dee Dee, of course she's colored, what else would she be?" "Why Mama I said, I thought she was a white baby." "Whatever made you think that?" Mama said?" "Because she is so light I said, and I thought God just gave you whatever baby He wanted you to have, so I thought He had sent us a little white baby." I then continued, "but Ma, if she is colored why is she so white?" To that, she replied, "she didn't stay in the oven long enough." There is a spiritual lesson we can all learn from Mama's response. Read on.

Stay in the Oven 'Til You are Done

Throughout life's journey, there will be times we find ourselves again, in the Potters Hand (Jeremiah 18:1-6). Those times when we will be "back on the wheel" of breaking and being remade into a greater vessel. These are the times when the Lord desires to enlarge our sanctuary, which is the temple of the Lord. This is the time the Lord desires to enlarge our borders and fill us with more of Himself and give us a greater anointing. We must be willing to be broken again, remade into a larger vessel, and then put into the oven by the Potter.

We must learn the lesson of "staying in the oven" (the refining furnace), until we are done (complete).

To come out before we are ready, only means we will have to do it all over again. Are you not tired of peat and repeat? Do you really enjoy taking life's character tests over and over and not passing? OK then, you must choose to stay in the oven until you are done.

The Face of an Older Sister

With the birth of my baby sister, our family consisted of five girls; the new **(white)** baby, and a seven, twelve, fourteen and fifteen year old. My eldest sister Mamie, who was eight years older than I, became our "Boss" because Mama had to work. Mama gave Mamie the orders and we had to follow them. She was like a second mother to my new baby sister and took very good care of her.

One summer day, we were all outside and Mamie was walking the baby who was then about 2 years old. She was dressed in a beautiful princess looking dress and was walking by herself. All of a sudden a teen-aged boy ran and scooped up my baby sister and began running with her. I jumped up very afraid that he was kidnapping her and I began to run after him shouting, "Give me back my sister, you'd better give me back my sister, what's wrong with you boy, give me back my sister." Mamie knew he was playing and she just stood there watching him run. Finally he stopped and gave her to me and I called him an unfriendly name, like stupid or dummy or dog or something. (After all, you had better not say anything stronger than that or the neighbors would tell Mama and need I say more?)

By this time my little sister was crying because she did not understand what was going on. I remember saying in my heart that I must always make sure nothing bad happens to her again. To this day, I still

33

feel like I must take care of Mama's baby. Over the years she has begged us to stop calling her "baby sister" and to please let her grow up. She is over 50 years old now and we are finally introducing her as our sister instead of our baby sister.

Yes, my older sister Mamie was our boss but she was also my protector. I always felt safe when she was around. Her face was a great blessing in my life. She was the sister who was willing to get up at night and escort me to the bathroom. You see, the house we stayed in was right next to a large Florist building which had been closed and torn down for years. It had turned into the neighborhood garbage dump, which was right in back of our house.

This garbage dump resulted in our house being a "place of blessing" for rodents, mice, rats and other crawling insects. I was so afraid to go to the bathroom at night because of the rodents that ran across the kitchen and bathroom floors. It may be hard to believe, but we had rats who were as big as cats. We had to turn the sugar and flour canisters upside down, so they could not take the tops off the canisters and get into the food.

I would wake Mamie up at night, (all of us slept in one bedroom) and she would take me to the bathroom. She would knock on the walls as we went through the living, dining and kitchen rooms. The mice and rats would then scatter when she turned the lights on. I had to hold up my legs as I sat on the commode because I was afraid a mouse would run over my feet.

Oh, how my sisters face was the place of blessing to me, when I was afraid. She would always say, "Don't be afraid Dee Dee, I'm with you." Sound familiar?

The word of the Lord tells us more than once that He will never leave us nor forsake us. What a comfort to hear someone on this side of heaven say this also.

Throughout my life until she passed away at the early age of 46, my sister Mamie's face was a place of encouragement to me. Over the years, we became a blessing to each other as we shared life's joys and sorrows. Where I was weak, she was strong and where she was weak, I was strong. We were there for each other. There is no one who could laugh like her. Her daughter laughs exactly like her and when I hear her laugh, it is like music to my ears.

Mamie was a woman that prayed a lot about everything. During those times I seldom attended Church because when I did go, all I did was cry. I just didn't feel good and didn't like the people to see me crying, but I just couldn't help it. When the choir began to sing the Lord's prayer, I would just weep because I wanted to be closer to God, but I was not comfortable going to church. I recall her telling me many times, "Dee Dee, you are going to be all right. I am praying for you and God is going to bring you closer to Himself. He is going to do it one day." Her prayers were answered in 1976 and one day we will rejoice together.

Don't Mess With Mamie's Food

As with most faces, Mamie's face was not always the place of blessing, especially when it came to someone "messing" with her food. Our portions of food consisted of one serving and maybe there was enough for someone to have two servings, depending on who finished first. I believe this is why I became good at math. I would come to the table and count how many rolls, doughnuts, chops or pieces of chicken were on the table. Then I knew how fast I had to eat my portion, so Mama would let me have some more to eat.

One Saturday morning, Mama was at work and we had doughnuts and milk for breakfast. We probably had eggs and bacon too. The sister who is the next oldest to me, grabbed the chocolate doughnut that belonged to Mamie and took a big bite out of it. She then laughed and mocked Mamie, as if to say, I have eaten your food and you cannot do anything about it.

Mamie's response, was not one of blessing but of wrath. She jumped up with a smile on her face and said..."Oh, so you're going to eat my doughnut are you? Well, I want it back right now." She then began choking my sister, until the doughnut came up.

Now I think I was about eight years old, and I thought Mamie was killing my sister. After the doughnut came up, the younger sister called Mamie "the N word" at which point, I thought death was surely on the way.

I ran next door to the lady's house (The Smith's) and said, "Please come quick, Mamie just choked my other sister and then she called her an "N" and I don't know what might happen if you don't come quick."

You see we were taught that to curse and fight was **not** a blessing and of course I was afraid that one of them would be killed. You see, I equated anger as a life threatening manifestation. Mamie was really, really angry.

I never wanted anyone to be angry with me, because the manifestation made me afraid for my life. I have always tried to please everyone and get everyone to like me so they would never be angry with me. Over the years, I have learned that I have been afraid of "bodily harm" most of my life. I have never liked any type of physical action that resulted in my body being hurt, including sports.

This resulted in me building walls of protection around me, so that others would not be able to "hurt, or kill me." In my relationships with the other gender, I was always afraid of saying or doing something that was not pleasing which might result in me being the object of physical violence.

I always knew that I could not tolerate violent relationships, because my mind thought, if you hit me, you want to hurt me and maybe you really want to kill me, thus I would have to fight for my life which might result in me killing you.

For many years, I was afraid of the slightest conflict because I took it to mean a threat to my life. Thus in any argument, I battled as though it was a war. I prepared myself to "win" and that was all there was too it. You see, it was a matter of life and death. It is difficult for me to remember a conflict that I did not win. Thank God for deliverance from every fear. He fights for me now.

All of my fears came as a result of someone's face, being something other than a blessing and a safe place. Needless to say, that day, I decided that I would never, ever, make Mamie angry and I would never ever "mess" with her food or anyone else's for that matter. Notice this was the same sister who was my protector and whose face was a blessing to my life as a young girl and young woman.

Over the years, the trials, stresses and tribulations of life, resulted in Mamie getting very sick. In spite of this, she was still able to work and provide a good home for her two children. She was a person that trusted in God and was able to conquer life's torments and fears. Her untimely death was the result of surgery. She remains alive in my heart as she left me many things to remember.

A Mother's Chastisement

Now when Mama came home and was told by the lady next door what had happened, Mamie had to reckon with Mama's face.

Mama's response to both sisters was "Oh, so you're going to choke your sister are you?" "Oh, so you're going to eat your sister's food are you?" Can I just tell you that her face was not a place of blessing to either one of them that day?

Can I just tell you that she was livid because the "neighbors" were aware that "her" well-behaved and well-trained girls were "acting out"? Can I just tell you how important it was back then to have control of your children and for them to have a good reputation in the neighborhood? I think that day, my mother's wishes were "burned" in their rumps and up beside their heads.

My mother was only about 5 feet 2 inches. We were all taller than her except for the sister that ate the chocolate doughnut. Mama did not let her height stop her or intimidate her. She would reach up and slap you and hit you on your backside or wherever. This little woman got her point across to you one way or another. Her desire was to bless you, but if you were not in agreement then you got the next best thing. It was rare when this happened and I guess I got more than any of the girls because of my outgoing personality and opinions.

Most times Ma did not have to chastise us in this manner. She usually used the art of verbal persuasion, reasoning with you, speaking to you with words of wisdom. However, if you did not believe fat meat was greasy, then she was well able to convince you that it was.

Questions/Reflections:

1. What childhood experiences have caused you to be afraid?

2. What kind of fears were they?

3. Did siblings, parents or other adults cause them?

4. How many siblings do you have and what gender?

5. What type of relationship do you have with each one?

6. Does reconciliation and/or restoration need to take place? In what way?

7. Are you willing to be the initiator?

Chapter Four:

The Face of Abandonment and Rejection

Feelings of Abandonment at
Three Years Old

Looking back over my childhood years, I believe I first encountered the *feeling* of abandonment at the age of three, when my mother took me to my grandmother's house for the week while she worked in the war plant.

I recall being in my grandmother's kitchen and my mother was getting ready to go. I even recall the red checkered table cloth on the big round kitchen table. It was a summer day on a Sunday afternoon. I recall laying my head on my mother's lap and crying and begging her not to leave me.

This went on for several minutes. Needless to say, she had to leave me anyway. The humorous thing about all this is that my Aunts told me that by the time Friday came and my mother picked me up to take me home for the week end, I cried and hollered again, only this time because I didn't want to leave Grandma's house. Go figure. Seriously, I really believe this was my first traumatic experience with feelings of abandonment.

Feelings of Abandonment at Twelve Years Old

The next time I believe I felt abandoned, was when my three older sisters all got married within a year of each other. I was only twelve years old and this left me alone to do "all" the household chores and shopping too.

The daily chores were to clean the living room, dining room, kitchen, bathroom and Mama's bedroom. In addition, sprinkle her heavily starched uniform until it was almost all wet and then iron it, until it could stand up on it's own. The ironing had to be done without a wrinkle or cat-face, as it was called back then, else I had to iron it again.

The daily house cleaning also included polishing all the furniture and sweeping the rugs. My baby sister was only five at that time and she didn't have to help me do any of the work. (Love bears all things… right? Right.)

Before my sisters married, my only chores were to daily clean the bathroom and dry the dishes. Is it any wonder that I felt like Cinderella during this time in my life? I did not think it was "fair" that as young as I was, I should have to do all this work, and shopping too. Every day I would cry for at least 15 minutes before I started my chores. I really felt unloved, abused and sorry for myself, which opened the door for teen-age rebellion.

The fact that I graduated at twelve years old to go to high school caused me to be around girls and boys 2-4 years older than myself. I began to hang out with the older kids and slightly rebel. I still graduated high school with honors at sixteen. Still much afraid of failure, bodily harm etc., I just acted out, until I was nineteen at which time I moved with one of my older sisters.

The Face of A Missionary

"DeLoris! You had better get in there and clean up that bathroom A number one, which meant it had better be done perfectly. This command came from my sister, who was next to the oldest. Even though my older sister Mamie was usually the "boss" when Mama was gone, we would still challenge her and sometimes not do what she said quickly. However, something inside of us knew that "this" sister was no one to play with.

She would tell you something once, in a firm but calm voice and you knew she meant it. There was something about this sister that was always serious, even though she was a lot of fun when we were growing up. She used to talk so much; her nickname was "mouth almighty." She was the one Mama relied on to take the money and buy the most groceries possible. Her diligence has caused her to prosper over the years.

Her face has always been one of helping you to help yourself. Telling you what to do and why. When she called me "DeLoris" instead of "Dee Dee," I knew not to talk back and to do whatever she said. She never had to holler or scream and has never liked to argue (I loved to debate all issues, commands, or instructions). To this day, if she is communicating with you and you even start to debate or argue, she says "just forget it."

She simply does not like to argue and debate. I have always loved to talk, debate, discuss, or whatever and have had to learn over the years that there is a time when "getting your point" across, is not the priority or purpose to an issue. At last, I have discovered, there is a time when we must "die" to our point, agenda and our self, in order to grow in the things of God.

This sister's face was one of encouragement and direction in my life. She was instrumental in setting up the interviews for the only two jobs I've had. One I worked at for 13 years and the other for 23 years. My second job ended up becoming an executive position. I thank my sister for opening the door and talking to the manager who agreed to interview me, even though I had been turned down by that same company a year before. I also thank her for commanding me "DeLoris, get down there and interview for this position."

My sister's face has always been one of a missionary, in that her face says, "I am a woman on a mission," whether she is shopping, studying, cooking, packing gifts for an overseas mission trip, praying, reading the word of God, or giving Godly counsel. Her husband's face is like a rear guard. His purpose? To protect her. She and her husband are givers and are missionaries at home and abroad, in the complete sense of the word. Their heart's desire is to serve and please the Lord.

She always loved to cook and invite the family over for Thanksgiving or Christmas dinner. When I was pregnant with Miss Rachel, she loved to cook for me. We have had many good years of laughter, prayer, counseling and love.

The Face of Sibling Conflict

My sister who was next to me, was almost five years older then I. When we were young, her face to me was sometimes the face of anger. She was also of very fair pigmentation (back then we called it "high yellow"), and she used to call me "black" when she got angry with me. I had the darkest skin of all my sisters. Black was not fashionable back then and was equated with the "N" word. To be called "black" was a fighting word at that time.

It seemed to me that she was always angry with me about one thing or another. We bickered a lot about little things, mostly when I was between seven and eleven years old.

She didn't like for me to read her funny books which were many. When I would sneak and read them anyway, she would fight me. I never put them back where I found them or in the order she had them because I forgot. She also did not like me to wear her nicely starched and ironed broomstick skirts. I was too young and dumb to know that she could tell I had worn them, because she hung them up with newspaper folded over the hangers and pinned them with safety pins. She could tell that there were new safety pin holes in the paper as well as the wrinkles in the skirts. She would then hit me again for wearing her clothes. Even though she was in high school and I was still in grammar school, I was big for my age and could get by wearing her clothes.

We would always fight at arms length, hitting one another in the "face" or trying to keep from getting hit. What we hated the most, is that Mama would then whip us for fighting and while we were crying from the whipping with tears and snot running down our noses, she would tell us "Now kiss each other and make up and say you are sorry."

Kissing each other was real punishment. Somehow, I always felt I really was sorry, but when I looked in her face, I never felt like she was really sorry. She still got mad at me whenever I read her funny books or wore her clothes or ribbons.

Most times when we got a whipping for fighting, she would get hers first. By the time I got mine, she was finished crying and when I would come out of the bedroom and still be crying, she would be waiting for me, laughing and pointing her finger at me saying "che, che, che, che, che, che, he, he, he, he, he" like a song. It was mockery at its best and hurt worse than the licks I got. It made me hurry and stop crying though, which was a good thing.

When I grew up enough to stay out of her clothes, things were much better between us and when she married and had children, I became her babysitter.

That is when we began to have a real sister to sister relationship. Our faces began to be a place of acceptance and love towards one another. We became very close, even dependent on each other and to this day we are the best of friends, talking to each other almost every day. Little did I know we would end up living together as adults.

The Face of Sibling
<u>Reconciliation and Acceptance</u>

I went to live with this sister when I was nineteen and she was left a widow at twenty-three with several children. Her husband died from open-heart surgery at the age of 25. I was ready to leave home and be on my own. It was a win win situation. She needed me and I needed her. Her house was just around the corner. During this time, our love for each other grew and grew. I watched her children while she attended church almost every night.

I loved to baby sit my nieces and nephews. They were more like my little sisters and brothers to me. They began calling me Mama Dee Dee. The youngest was only eight months old when his father died. We used to tease him and confuse him as to who his mother was. He looked a lot like me because his skin color was closer to mine. By then I was working and used to love to buy clothes and toys for them. I witnessed at 19 years old, the face of my sister, a widow.

The Face of a Widow

My sister's husband had only been dead six months when I moved in with her. There were many times her face was one of sorrow, grief and dismay. She never talked or complained about her husband being gone. She buried herself in her children and poured all her love into them. They became her reason for living.

She had recently become a "Pentecostal" believer and used to pray in "other tongues" all the time. I watched as she continued to cry out to the Lord in tears. I knew that she was looking to the Lord for answers, comfort, strength and healing of her broken heart.

We used to call people that prayed like her, "sanctified." We also believed that the only people who could pray like that were those that gave up all their habits, like drinking, smoking, dancing, wearing make-up, sexual immorality and the like, so they could be "sanctified."

There were times that I felt I could understand what she was saying to God. It seemed as though, she was sometimes asking Him why He "took" her husband and left her with five children. Other times it seemed she as saying "Oh Lord, I thank you for my children, I thank you for taking care of us, I thank you for revealing yourself to me. You are my Messiah, Though you slay me, yet will I trust you." "O God, help me to raise all my children and provide for them. Bless me to live to see them grown

and serving you." "Oh Messiah, Messiah, Messiah....
You are Lord of all!"

Even though I sometimes felt I understood her
prayers in other tongues, I never let it really touch
me. I was not ready to become too "religious." I was
afraid to make promises to God and not keep them.
I was also afraid of things like bodily harm from
men, sickness, pain, trials and tribulations and even
death if I made God angry. So I simply tried to live
by the golden rule...do unto others.

I was afraid to truly seek "the face" of God, because
I was not aware that His Face was and is "the place
of blessing." It has taken many years for me to
discover the purpose of God's face and our face,
which is to extend blessings.

I lived with my sister for a year and then moved
into a three-room apartment directly across the
street. Her "face" had become a blessing in my
life. We became close sisters and friends, laughing,
crying and blessing one another with our face. I was
overjoyed because I knew then that my sister really
loved me.

Chapter Five:

The Faces of My Heart

A Husband for Me

My husband's face was a place safety and liberty most of the time. He never demanded that I do this or that or not do this or that. His philosophy was, "I'm grown, you're grown, you do what you want to do and I'll do what I want to do." "If you want to buy carpeting or furniture, do it. If I want to buy records and equipment or cars, I'll do it. We're both grown and working and can pay for whatever we want." I am not saying that this is the best way to have a relationship, but I loved not being controlled and told what to do. Yet, I was still afraid of not pleasing him, for fear he might get angry with me.

I believe that there is something deep down in the female that is "afraid" of making the male(s) in her life angry. This can result in a hidden fear of bodily harm, especially if a female has been the object of violence by a male. I was not afraid of my husband, but I worried myself about being sure he did not get angry with me. I just wanted to please him in every way.

I was afraid of being hit or hurt if he became angry, based on relationship conflicts I had heard about, witnessed and experienced prior to marrying my husband.

49

We usually saw eye to eye on most things. However, we were never on the same page when it came to what we wanted to achieve in life. Unfortunately for me, his Utopia was my starting point. I loved to be at home and he loved to be out with his friends. He loved music and was a disc jockey on the weekends. He was a long-distance trucker and was usually gone from 3-5 days at a time. He was also the last of the big time spenders. Needless to say, we had issues with regard to how the money should be spent.

When he would come home, he wanted to be out with his friends. Of course, I wanted him to be at home with us. I wanted a new home in the suburbs and to own our own semi-truck cab. He wanted to be able to rent a high-rise apartment along the lake. He loved the nightlife with its glitter and activity. This was his definition of success, although it never came to pass.

I wanted to save money and he loved to spend money, especially on others. He just loved to "put everyone's food and drink on his tab." He loved people and always wanted to be around them, laughing and partying and just being what he called "happy." He loved to be the life of the party wherever he went.

Still, his face was one of blessing as he came through the door and called out "RACHELLLLL." Yes, our daughter Rachel, was his total pride and joy. She loved to see his face, smiling, laughing and approving of all she said or did.

Rachel was the bond that kept us together. He used to say, "By the time she is seven years old, she will think the sun rises and sets on me." He treated her like a princess and always pushed her to do more and excel in everything she did. She was his reason for being and he always called her "beautiful" and promised her a big diamond when she graduated from high school.

For the most part we got along well, except for those times when he would stay out for the week-end and I would get mad, or those times we argued about how the money should be spent.

I recall one time, when we were in a heated argument (I did most of the hollering and screaming), he would say, "I don't want to hear all of this noise" or "Dee Dee, how long are you going to keep this up?" "I am getting tired of listening to you make all this noise. I can't stand much more of this!" I perceived from the way he looked at me, over the top of his reading glasses, that I had just about gone too far, because he said, "You had better be glad that I do not think of you as "just a woman," but as "Rachel's Mother." I immediately calmed down and thought, "Thank you God for Rachel." I am happy to say my husband never raised his hand to me, no matter how upset I became.

Most of the time, when I argued, he would just laugh and say, "Boy, boy, boy, here we go again. Dee Dee, you are too nervous and jealous. You need to calm down and stop worrying about everything and everybody. Girl, you cannot dictate to me, because I am a man and I will do what I want, not what you say."

Then, there were those times, when his face was one of blessing, approval, love and even pride towards me. He always wanted me to "dress up" just to go to the grocery store on weekends, even though he wore his work clothes. The look on his face when he introduced me to others was one to behold. When he said,"This is my wife, Dee Dee," you would have thought I was the Queen of Sheba. His entire face would light up and even blush with a sense of accomplishment, as if to say, "Look at this beautiful woman who is in love with me!" There was no doubt in my heart that he was proud to say that I was his wife. He loved to smile at me and call me his sophisticated woman.

He didn't speak words of love very often, but he would just look at me and his eyes and his quiet smile said, "I love you and knowing you love me, makes me feel 10 feet tall." It's like pulling teeth to get some men to say, "I love you."

Sometimes I would say to him, "Jimmy Babe, I love you." Can I just tell you that his response was not "I love you too," but instead it was "Thank you." "Thank you?" "Thank you?" Then I would say to him, "Sweetheart, that is not the appropriate response." To which he would then reply, "I love you too...in my own way." "In your own way? Just what does that mean?" In my heart I guess I always knew he was saying that he loved me too, even though like many men, he could not express it in words the way I wanted him to. So I learned to accept the truth. Love is really actions that speak even louder than words.

All of this to say, the face of my husband is one my daughter Rachel and I have never forgotten. He died from Cancer in 1978 at the age of 42, much too young for a man that was so full of life and love for others, especially his Rachel.

The Loss of a Mother and Friend

From 1964 until 1976, Mama and I lived together, until she went home to be with the Lord. There is a scripture in the book of Isaiah, Chapter 6 verse one, that says, "In the year that King Uzziah died, I (Isaiah) saw the Lord." Let me just say, that in the year 1976, my Mother, who had become my best friend, confidant, counselor, encourager, and helper, died, I saw (my need) for the Lord.

Up to that point, I had no desire to attend church on a regular basis, other than the Holidays. I was baptized at the age of twelve, and attended Sunday school and church regularly until I was around 16 years old and began to see many hypocrites and lost my trust in the "people/leaders" in the church. In spite of this, I did not lose my faith that there was a God and that he loved me.

I decided that I could live according to the "golden rule," which was in the bible and therefore, did not have to attend church. I felt that those in trusted positions, preached, prayed and taught one thing, while they practiced another.

But when my Mother died, I saw my need for the Lord, regardless of what others were doing or had done. Even though some were hypocrites, I still needed to draw closer to God, seek HIS FACE and not be afraid. I needed to know more about the One who created me. I never wanted God to consider me a hypocrite and since I knew I was not perfect, I was sometimes afraid of going to church. We always heard our parents talk about God striking you down dead and that He was "no one to play with." Therefore, I stayed away from church. I did not want to pretend I was obedient to all that was written in the Bible. Neither did I want God to consider me a liar or be angry with me and strike me dead. How sad to have this concept of the God of our Salvation who loves us and gave His life for us.

My basic motive for seeking the face of God was this; I wanted to be sure, that I would see my Mother's face again. I made a promise at her funeral, that I would see her again. I did not know how to accomplish this, except to do as the old spiritual Mothers used to say and sing..."Just a closer walk with thee."

Rachel's Face – Sunshine, Courage, Faith & Love
<u>The Face of Sunshine</u>

She was the most beautiful baby I had ever seen. This little bundle of joy that the Doctor said was mine, had silky curly black hair that was layered as though she had just come from the hair salon. When I saw her fair skin, I thought "how could she be so light? I did not imagine I would have a light skinned baby, because I felt I was too dark. Well, the hand of heritage reached back and this little baby was fair. Her face was like sunshine and joy.

We named her or rather my Mother requested that she get to name her. Ma said, "I did not get to name any of my girls, so will you let me name this one?" How could I say no to Mama? So she named her Rachel Angela.

Had I only known what the name Rachel meant, I would have fought harder to name her something else. Rachel means lamb and spiritually her life has been like that of The Lamb, as regards physical suffering. Her middle name, Angela means, messenger of God and I would not that change for anything.

Yet, God knew all along and foreordained that her name would be Rachel. This has brought both she and I much comfort during her times of suffering.

From the time they placed Rachel in my arms, even to this day, she has been a joy to my soul. She has faced life's circumstances and trials with great strength, enthusiasm, courage and joy. Yes, my beloved Rachel has had many physical valleys to walk through and yet she has been instrumental in teaching me how to become an overcomer.

When I was in my twenties and thirties, my thoughts and heart were filled with all kinds of fear. Fear of failure, hunger, poverty, mockery, abuse, you name it, I had it. I was so afraid to drive a car for fear I might have an accident or even be ticketed by the Police. I feared others finding out about it, which would make me the laughing stock in town. I know now these fears were unhealthy thoughts and came from a mentality of fear because of past experiences.

I will always love Rachel, because as a very young girl of eight years old, she would give me wise counsel and encourage me not to be afraid.

When Rachel was five years old, she was diagnosed with Petit Mal epilepsy, which is a seizure disorder and when it strikes, it puts the person in a semi-conscious state and they cannot respond to others.

She would have these seizures from 10 – 20 times a day and they could last from 20 seconds to a minute. She had just entered kindergarten and many of the children as well as some of the teachers did not understand this condition. Rachel also had developed a physical problem with her weight. By the time she was eleven she was extremely overweight. Needless to say she suffered mockery, ridicule and persecution from her peers and even from those who claimed to be her friends.

Still during this time, she was able to impart to me the wisdom and courage she had to draw on, as she faced life's challenges. I recall once when she was eight years old and I was in the dining room, crying about something, Rachel came out of her bedroom and said to me, "Mommy, you can cry, but you do not have to let the tears come to your eyes." Years later, I realized how she coped with the mockery and unkind words of other children. She had learned how to cry on the inside(which is really not good for you). We must learn to "listen" to our children when they speak.

Another time, I recall shaking like a leaf when I was driving and our car was the first car at an angled intersection. I did not know which light was my light. I actually started trembling and gasping, saying, "Rachel, I don't know which light is mine." "Oh God, what am I going to do?" Rachel's calm response at age 12 was, "Take it easy Mommy, it's going to be OK. You can do it. Just look straight ahead. Your light is the one straight ahead of you. Don't be scared Mommy, you can do it."

Walking the Aisle

This is the true story of my life. My Rachel, giving me courage through the years to trust the Lord. My Rachel, the one who actually started me on the path back to the church and God two years before my Mother died. One day she came home from church and said, "Mommy, Mommy, I almost walked down the aisle today." Now, "walking the aisle," meant to join the church and be baptized. My response to her was, "Look Rachel, you cannot walk the aisle yet. When you are baptized, your parents are supposed to be with you. I'm going to get myself together pretty soon and come back to church. Until then, you cannot walk the aisle. You have plenty of time for that, you are still very young."

The next week, while walking the blocks from the train to my job, I heard a voice within me say "Suffer the little children and forbid them not to come unto me, for of such is the Kingdom of Heaven." Let me tell you that the fear of almighty God came upon me. I knew this was the Lord, because I had stopped going to church years ago and was not one that knew the scriptures by heart.

That evening when I came home from work, I talked with Rachel and kindly said to her, "Honey, the next time you feel something inside of you that makes you want to "walk the aisle," well, you just do it. It will be okay." (I really thought that she would not "feel" the spirit of God for maybe another 3-4 years.)

The very next Sunday, Rachel came running in the house, "Mommy, Mommy, I did it, I did it, I walked the aisle today and I'm going to be baptized in water on next Sunday." I was speechless and surprised but I simply said, "That's nice Rachel." "Now what all do I have to buy to get you ready for next Sunday." Inside I was saying, "How am I ever going to be able to go to church to witness this event. It is so hard for me to sit there without feeling so bad and crying."

I did not know about conviction, only condemnation, so it was difficult for me to understand why I cried and why I felt so bad when I occasionally went to church. Suffice it to say, that I did go with Rachel to witness her baptism and officially becoming a member of the church even though she was still very young.

When she crossed both of her arms across her heart, the Pastor prayed over her and she went down in the water. I then began to scream out loud, "Help me Jesus. Please help me Lord." I began to sob uncontrollably as I felt myself surrendering all of my fears, anxieties and shortcomings to the Lord. I began to cast all my cares on Him. I began to feel his love and peace come over me.

When the Altar call was done at the end of the service, I got up from my seat and ran to the front of the Church and fell in the arms of the Pastor. "I've come back home, I've finally come back home," I said to him. That day I rejoined the church after being gone approximately 18 years, except for Holidays. Yes, once again, my Rachel was used as an instrument to give me courage to face the Truth. Jesus said, "I am the way, the truth and the life."

The years went by and God was faithful to Rachel and to me. He healed her of both Petit Mal and Grand Mal seizures (which she began to have at age 11). He healed her weight problems and she was no longer overweight. She was sanctified by the Lord at age 13 and filled with the Holy Ghost and fire. Rachel began to minister as a young teenager in Church with the youth and sang in the choir and special music ensemble. She became a Sunday school teacher and was a youth Camp Counselor for many years.

The Face of Courage

During her teenage years, Rachel helped me trust in the agape/unconditional love of God. Each time she had an opportunity to do the "normal" things like driving a car or playing on the baseball, basketball and volleyball teams, I had to go through deliverance from fear. I recall saying to her, "Rachel, Mommy cannot let you take driving lessons. I could not live with myself if you had a seizure and got killed while driving. Please don't ask me to do this, I just can't, I can't." Her response was as usual, one of great faith, "Mommy, Mommy, don't you know that God is taking care of me? Don't you know that He is going to be with me? Don't you know that He will not let anything happen to me that would hurt me or anyone else? Mommy, you have to believe, you have to trust, you have to give me to God. Mommy, don't be scared."

After much crying and sobbing and asking the Lord to help me believe, I finally gave my permission for Rachel to learn to drive. Her doctor was in agreement, as it had been a long time since she had been sick because of seizures.

Bless God, she learned to drive and then I had to go through deliverance again, when it was time for her to drive without me in the car. Each time she stepped into a new season, I had to cry out and surrender her to God. Often I was condemned because of "Oh ye of little faith" that is written in the scriptures.

A Spiritual Faith Lesson

One morning when Rachel dropped me off at the train station, I noticed her eyes looked a little funny. I began to fear. When she drove off down the street, I could see her car from the platform. I began to pray, "Lord, please forgive me for being afraid, please don't let her have a seizure while she is driving. Please Lord; don't let the thing I fear the most, come upon her. I am trying not to be afraid, but Lord you are the only one I can turn to. Please help my unbelief; please don't be angry with me for not having more faith. Lord please take care of my Rachel."

I will never ever forget the response of the Lord. He gave me a quick lesson in faith. He began to speak to my heart, "DeLoris, the evidence of faith is not based only on what you say or feel. It is really based on what you do" (the actions that you take). When Abraham offered up Isaac, it was faith based on action. His action said what he really believed and that was "The Lord will provide." The Spirit of God went on to say, "Even though you feel you are not walking in faith because of the feelings of fear and dread in your mind, each day you still give her the keys to the car. Each day you release her into my hands. You are not doubting in your heart. You are having these thoughts in your mind but you are putting into action what you believe in your heart. This is faith in action."

"Each time DeLoris, when you give Rachel the keys to the car you are actually offering her up to me. You are actually believing 'The Lord will provide Himself a Lamb.'" I account your actions as righteousness, just as I accounted Abraham's. No longer are you to condemn yourself because of the emotions that come upon you concerning Rachel. No longer shall you let others ridicule you and say you have no faith, because you do not throw away her medicine."

"Go to work, release your tears and your fears, and do not condemn yourself ever again concerning your faith. Just know that faith, is what you do, not just what you think or say. Be at peace dear one, Rachel is in the palm of my hand."

Since that day, many years ago, I have been at peace, because the Lord revealed to me the truth about what He considers faith in God. I have since "offered" Rachel up many times, in faith believing and trusting that "God will provide Himself a Lamb."

A Cross For Rachel

In 1996 after overcoming other physical trials, including three major surgeries between 1992 and 1995, Rachel was then diagnosed with cardiomyopathy, which resulted in her receiving a defibrillator/pacemaker implant device(ICD).

The purpose of this device is to restart your heart in the event it stops beating or regulate your heartbeat in the event the irregularity could be fatal. It electrically shocks the heart several times in 5 or 6 second intervals. Needless to say, this is very painful and traumatic.

It takes a lot of courage, faith and trust in God, to endure physical issues, time and time again and not lose your faith and hope for the future. Rachel has always had the gift of faith, given to her by the Lord. She has more courage in her little finger than I have in my entire body.

Since 1996 her defibrillator has "fired/shocked" her five times, two because of incorrect program settings. It is not a pleasant thing to witness, because the electrical shock is painful and frightening. Some have said, "It is like being kicked in the chest by a horse." The defibrillator will continue to fire/release an electrical shock, every 6 seconds for 6 times in a row, trying to either restart or regulate an irregular heartbeat.

The first time it fired on her was Christmas of 1996. The first shock caused her to scream at which point I came running into the family room. Rachel had actually been praising God in the dance, which was unusual for her (dancing). She had just had surgery in November and was giving thanks to God for keeping her alive.

She had been hoping the device would never have to "fire," especially while she was conscience. Being a Nurse made it difficult for her in that she knew too much about her condition. She just had enough time to scream "Mommy, it went off," when another shock came. This time I saw her face. I then understood for the first time what the face of Jesus must have looked like when the nail was driven in his feet and hands. I believe I saw the joy of the enemy of our souls. The one who came to steal, kill and destroy. I recall screaming "Satan, the Blood of Jesus." Rachel then fell to the ground with another shock.

I began to say to her the things she used to say to me. I began to tell her she was going to be all right as I breathed in her mouth. I began to call on Jesus to come and regulate her heartbeat. We then called 911 and the ambulance came and took her to the hospital. We discovered that her device had been programmed too low and did not allow for the heart activity that follows dancing.

Her most recent need for faith and courage came in September 2004 when her defibrillator "fired" again. Her heart had gone into a true irregular heartbeat.

Had it not been for the Lord and the device, Rachel would be with the Lord. Thank God for medical technology. She has been off work building up her heart muscle for several months now. The Lord has miraculously healed and is continuing to heal her heart. Even through this trying time in her life, Rachel's face is glowing more than ever before. She has seen the One who conquered the face of death. She has allowed His face to shine upon her and give her peace. Like Sarah, Rachel has counted the Lord as faithful, reliable and true to His Word (Hebrews 11:11).

Most people do not understand the emotional trauma that is associated with looking into the face of death. Most people do not understand that more than the physical body burns resulting from the ICD shock need to be healed. The mind and the emotions also need to be touched by God and those who love you.

Strength To Endure

I believe that the Lord put "Extra Strength" tablets of courage, faith, hope and love in the heart of this one called Rachel. When she was a baby and received her shots, she would not really cry, but instead put her lips together, arch her back and say "oomph." Her pediatrician then said, "This is a tough baby." I am a firm believer that God puts into us the measure of strength/toughness we need to face, overcome and conquer the obstacles of this life. It would be good if we all believed this, so that when trouble comes we would be able to say to ourselves, "I can take this, because God put the "stuff" in me that I need to get through this. With His help, I can do and go through all things."

More Than A Conqueror

Rachel has become a woman of faith in the Word of God, which she studies diligently and has been used by the Lord to teach others. She is a woman of integrity and honor that believes prayer changes circumstances and people. Her face is and always has been a blessing. A face that comes into someone's presence to release love, healing, esteem and grace. She is the best thing that ever happened to me outside of the Lord. I have always said to her, "Always know that if your only purpose in life was to be born to help Mommy get on the path of eternal like, just know that your life has already had great meaning."

The Lord has blessed Rachel to become more than a conqueror. Her life is a living testimony that "no thing (trials or tribulations), shall be able to separate her from the love of God, which is in Christ Jesus, her Lord. (Romans 8:35-38)

Rachel is trusting God for her Boaz, (husband), whom we know will come in the Lord's timing. In the meantime, she is content to be a vessel of honor for God, who uses her life prophetically in singing, teaching, healing, and providing wise counsel to others. We have both had the privilege of ministering God's love and word together, to the Nations at home and abroad.

I love to hear Rachel speak and teach the scriptures. Often she tells her audience, "Me and Mommy, well, we grew up together." (And that's the truth!) Like the Apostle Paul once said, so do we both say, "We are what we are *(and where we are)*, by the Grace of God." Our personal praise declaration is "Can we just say, 'Thank You Jesus.'"

My Personal Search for
<u>God & The Promise</u>

When Rachel "Walked the Aisle" and was baptized, it brought me back to Church. I began to read the bible and search the gospels. Then my mother died and I began to be consumed with reading the New Testament Gospel and the Epistles. I began to believe what I had read. I began to understand that the promise of the Holy Spirit was for all who believed and it was not based on what denomination you were from or what church you attended.

One day I said to the Lord, "I am in so much pain and sorrow from the loss of my mother, it does not seem like I can recover. I think I want to be "sanctified," and receive "the promise" i.e., to be filled with the Holy Spirit of God, speaking with tongues of fire as the bible speaks of (Acts 1:4-5; 2:1-4)."

After reading and searching the scriptures for another year and a half, Jesus looked over His word and performed it in my life. He baptized and filled me with the Holy Ghost and fire in my bedroom the evening of December 16, 1977. The manifestation of His Spirit was upon me for four hours. I spoke with other tongues and prophesied and interpreted in English what I was saying in other tongues, as the Holy Spirit gave me the utterance and the interpretation.

During those four hours, the Spirit of the Lord was upon me for healing, cleansing, deliverance, prophecy, revelation, holy fear and joy. It was as though the Face of the Lord was shining on me with His Face and imparting to me His Love, Forgiveness, Safety, Salvation, Peace and Joy.

I could actually feel the sorrow, fear and heart-break that rested under my left breast, leave my body as the Holy Spirit filled me up with rivers of living water. I felt the acceptance of God the Father, as the Lord Jesus Christ baptized me according to His word written in the book of Matthew 3:11.

I felt all my fears being replaced by His Love, Mercy and Grace. I felt condemnation leave as He poured in His Love and washed me in His Blood. It was the most awesome and beautiful thing, to experience the presence of the Lord in this way. Truly, I was sealed unto the day of redemption on that night. The Face of God that I used to fear, became that night, The Face of Blessing in my life.

These Five Chapters, have been a short summary of a few of the faces that have shaped my life. Many positive seeds were sown into my life by those whose who allowed their faces to be a blessing. The seeds sown into my being were, love, integrity, courage, faithfulness and determination, and gave purpose to my life. These were the seeds that helped me to overcome and uproot the many negative seeds that had also been sown by those unpleasant faces.

The negative seeds sown into my mind, heart and emotions as a result of the faces of others that were NOT a blessing **were**:

Fear, abandonment, rejection, confusion, anger, resentment, low esteem, rebellion, spirit of perfection, pride, and unforgiveness.

Thank God for His Face of Blessing, Relationship, Intimacy and Truth, through which I have been forgiven, filled, healed, delivered and set free. YES! !

The next few Chapters, will address the revelation of the "Aaronic Blessing" given by the Lord in Numbers 6:22-27. This blessing, is what I believe, the Lord originally intended our faces to impart to others as well as receive from others.

It is my hope, that after reading the remaining chapters, you will look at your face and everyone else's face in a new and exciting way. Hopefully, you will fully understand just why God gave you your face. Hopefully, you will discover the joy of allowing your face to be "the place of blessing" for others.

Chapter Six:

Your Face – The Place of Blessing

The Aaronic Blessing

"And the Lord said to Moses. Say to Aaron and his sons, This is the way you shall bless the Israelites." "Say to them, the Lord bless you and watch, guard and keep you: The Lord make His face to shine upon and enlighten you and be gracious (kind, merciful, and giving favor) to you:" "The Lord lift up His (approving) countenance upon you and give you peace (tranquility of heart and life continually). And they shall put My name upon the Israelites, and I will bless them." (Numbers 6:22-27,Amplified)

The Face of Relationship and Intimacy

The revelation for this book came as a result of doing a study on Relationship. The face is the part of the body that actually determines what kind of relationship there will be between two or more people. True relationship cannot be achieved without "the face." Without the face, we cannot relate one to another. I cannot look at your elbow or waist or foot and discern your needs. I must look into your eyes if I want to see your soul and understand who you are.

Statistics show that one of the greatest fears of mankind is speaking in front of other people. This could be restated as speaking in front of other "faces." After all, for the most part, the face is the only thing beside the hands that is constantly visible to others. The rest of the body is usually covered.

So then, we are not afraid of people per se, but we are afraid of their "faces." No wonder, Jeremiah 1:8 states, "Do not be afraid of their faces, for I am with you to deliver you, says the Lord."

The original intent of God was for the face of mankind to reveal his image and likeness. Meaning, that the face would bless, shine upon, extend grace, give approval, accept, encourage, and lift up others. Why then is the average person afraid of the faces of others? The reason is that in reality, the face is the place where you and I may have received cursing, rejection, mockery, fear, verbal abuse, dis-approval, disdain, scorn and everything BUT the blessing.

> For many, if not most people, the face has often been the place that has awakened every negative emotion that can be felt, rather than vice-versa.

What makes the face so powerful? It's components. Let's take a look at what the face is comprised of.

The Components of The Face

The face is described as the Head, containing the eyes, ears, nose and mouth. Let us identify the face as, "The Place of Blessing, Relationship, Intimacy and Truth." The complete face is basically, the place of truth. It is where the rubber meets the road. Although it is possible to hide the truth, more often than not, if you understand the components of the face, you can usually look into the expression of the face and either the truth will be revealed or the lie will be exposed.

The Eyes of The Face

It is said, that the "eyes" of the face reveal the soul of a man. The major components of your soul are your mind/intellect, emotions/feelings and will/ desires/choices.

If you look into someone's eyes with the purpose of seeing their "soul," the **truth** about what they are feeling, thinking and desiring, can often be discerned. You will be able to see what it is they "need," as you look into their face and then, **your** face can become a "place of blessing" to them, as you open up your heart and respond to their need. Your face could respond in many ways.

Maybe they simply need a smile or a word of encouragement or just need to see a face that seems to say, "I'm concerned, I care," or "I'm approachable, you can talk to me." Or "May I be a shoulder, or a bridge over troubled waters for you?"

However, if you are afraid of their faces, you will not be able to look into their eyes, and discern their needs. Often parents say to their children when they want them to tell the truth, "Look into my eyes." This usually works, because it is most difficult to look into the eyes of the soul and not respond with truth. It takes much practice to look someone directly in their eyes and lie.

Just as words can pierce the heart and soul, it is the eyes, that accept or reject, or impart love, hate or indifference. It is the eyes, that either send darts of death or put the scepter of life out. It is the eyes, that open or close the door to true relationship. It is the eyes, that often intimidate and cause great fear to come upon someone.

Notice, the words intimate, timid and intimidate are very close together. The purpose of intimidation is to make you timid through fear, and fight any possibility of true intimacy and relationship, which is your God given destiny. Our eyes often speak much louder than words. They can pierce, injure and draw blood, just like words. The eyes are the ones that give you "the look."

How many times have you heard someone say, "If looks could kill, I'd be dead" or "He/she looked at me like "drop dead""?

Your eyes were created to see what God sees and send to others His message of love, forgiveness, acceptance, long suffering, esteem, encouragement, joy, laughter and positive blessings. How powerful a "look" can be. It can make or break a person's spirit and even change the course of their destiny.

The Nose of The Face

The nose, is one of the most important parts of the face, in that it is used not only to smell, but to breathe in oxygen which supplies life to the blood that flows to all our cells and organs. There are so many different kinds of noses. I like to think of noses as the "tool of discernment." Good and evil has a smell. Good has a sweet smelling scent and evil has a putrid scent like death. Our noses were created to allow us to breathe in the breath of life and to smell the scent of good and evil or life and death. There is a saying "he/she can smell a rat, a mile away." These are people who have the gift of discernment and can identify the motives and intents of the heart, both good and evil.

The "unaccepted or mocked nose, lips, eyelids, chin, and or ears" has impacted millions of people, many even obtaining plastic surgery to change their facial features. Untold millions of others cannot afford surgery and often end up becoming merciless; mocking and rejecting others who face the same mockery.

The Mouth of the Face

The mouth, is the most powerful component of the face. It gives voice to the eyes, nose and ears. It speaks for the spirit, soul and body.

The mouth of the face is also the **creative** part of the face, in that it is the component that "speaks words" and causes things to come into existence, whether good or evil, negative or positive, natural or spiritual.

In Genesis chapter one, everything that God created was "spoken" into existence and then it came to pass. "Let there be," was spoken and whatever followed "Let there be," was created. God called those things that "be not, as though they were" and they came into being and existence like He called it.

When your mouth speaks words, it is the same as saying "Let there be." When your mouth speaks words against others, you are not only creating a negative situation for someone else, but you are indirectly calling for the same judgment or words to be activated in your own life and circumstances. (Matthew 7:1-2).

We must begin to understand that **our words are seeds** that are sown, the moment we speak them. Those seeds/words are not only what we give or sow into others, but we too will eat of the harvest that comes forth from the seeds we have sown, whether they be good or bad, life or death, joy or sorrow.

PLEASE, get this: ***You are planting the crop you will eat next year and in the years to come, by the words that you speak today, about others or about yourself.*** Often a seed takes more than one year to bring forth its fruit. Some trees only bear fruit every two or three years. It is written, "You shall eat the fruit of your lips (Proverbs 18:20)."

It may take as long as 20 years, but eventually you will eat of the fruit of your lips. When I was in my early twenties, I was not walking in wisdom and truth, although I believed what others had said about me since I was little. I was always told that I was smart and wise beyond my years. So, just like most people, I eventually believed the commercials that had been spoken about me.

When I was 19, I began to have female problems. The doctor discovered a cyst on one of my ovaries. It caused me great pain during my menstrual cycle. A few years later, I was chatting with my friends and we were talking about our female problems, birth control, babies and such.

I chimed in and said something like, "Well, I doubt that I will have to worry about this my whole life, since I will probably have a hysterectomy by the time I'm 40 years old. I made that statement in my early twenties. So, who was on the operating table having a hysterectomy at 40? Do I need to tell you? Do you have to guess? I think not, of course it was yours truly.

This is a perfect example of speaking/sowing negative seeds, even about your own self. Although spoken in jest, I still ate of the fruit of my lips. Scripture admonishes us to "Put away foolish jesting." The Psalmist wrote:

> *"Let the words of my mouth and the meditations of my heart be acceptable in thy sight Oh Lord, my strength and my Redeemer (Psalm 19:14)."*

We must be slow to speak and make sure that the words that leave our mouth are not only acceptable to God, but also to us. Had I used this as a rule of thumb, I would have thought, "Is a hysterectomy acceptable to me? Is this what I really want to happen to me? If not, then I must not speak it into existence."

What do you do, if the words leave your mouth before you realize what you have spoken into existence? Then you must "pull them down to the ground." Uproot them, in the name of Jesus and pull them down to the ground. Condemn them from prospering against you, cursing them at the root, so they will not bear fruit. Isaiah 54:17 tells us that we can condemn every tongue that has risen up against us in judgment. This includes words of judgment that have been spoken, even by your own tongue.

Depending on the condition of the root or seed, some trees are barren and never bear fruit, even though they look like other trees and have branches and leaves.

Jesus cursed the fig tree and we must use this same principle to arrest words/seeds that have left our mouth when we suddenly realize that the harvest or fruit of those seeds are unacceptable to the Lord and would also be to us.

The Will, The Choice and
The Tongue of the Face

We must discipline ourselves to think, before we speak. Be slow to speak. Consider your ways and your words. Proverbs 18:21 teaches us that the power of death and life are in the tongue.

The book of Deuteronomy 30:19, reveals to us that the greatest power we have is the power of choice. The choice of life or death is continuously before us. Each second, minute and hour of every day, whether we realize it or not, we are choosing whom we will serve. Are you aware of the choices you are making by the second, minute, hour and day? Do you take the time to evaluate the component of your soul, your will/desires, which result in your final decisions and choices?

Do you not know, that every action or deed, is the direct result of a choice and the end of that choice will bring forth life or death, blessing or curse, fruitfulness or barrenness, success or failure? All of this, is based on your understanding the greatest power you have within you. "C H O I C E."

Allow me to have a play on the word choice. Isn't it interesting that the last three letters in choice phonetically say "I see"? The first three letters are the same as in the word "Choose." Our lives would totally be different, if we said, I will no longer be quick to choose until "I see."

See what? **See** how the thoughts and plans of the Lord will fit into my choices. **See** what the will of God is at this point in time for my life. **See** if my choices fit in with His global plan. **See** how they fit into His Kingdom.

What if, on an hourly, daily basis, you would begin to think "Yes, I have the power to choose, but I will wait until "*I See*."" "I will not make this decision until *I see* (have considered) what the end may be."

I am not saying you should know the outcome before you make a decision, but I am saying, that you should at least consider the outcome. Often the end of a thing can be seen and known, if we would evaluate it based on the principle of life or death, blessing or cursing and seek direction from God. John 16:13 indicates, that The Spirit of Truth will guide you and show you things to come.

Most of us have more than one example of errors in our choices, that had they been thought out beforehand, we would have chosen differently. This includes every area of our lives, such as our words, actions, deeds, and responses to circumstances and relationships.

The mouth/tongue of the face, is the only thing in this world that cannot be tamed by man. The mouth/tongue can only be tamed by the Spirit of God. The book of James chapter three, speaks volumes about the tongue that abides in the mouth. The tongue is said to be unruly, full of deadly poison and is set on fire by hell itself. Read it for yourself. You may be enlightened on how the Lord feels about corrupt communication, profanity, vulgarity and cursing others.

James goes on to say, that the tongue is the only member that blesses God and curses men, who are made after the similitude of God. Could this mean that we are unaware that when we curse men, we are indirectly cursing God, because He made mankind after His own image and likeness? Think about this seriously.

The Lord through James asks us the questions; "Does a tree bring forth both good and bad fruit?" "Does a spring send forth fresh water and bitter from the same opening? Does it yield both salt water and fresh? "

"Does a fig tree bear olives or a grapevine bare figs?" God is saying "Don't you get it?" "Out of the "same" mouth proceeds both blessing and cursing." James goes on to say "...this conflict should not be (James 3:3-10)." ***Please, please do not receive any condemnation, just think about this and allow your heart to be cleansed and changed for the better, so that you will no longer allow your emotions to release/sow negative seeds through your mouth.***

Consider The Power of Your Words

Do the words/seeds that you speak/sow have good fruit bearing purposes?

Do you really understand that your words will bring forth a harvest in kind?
(Negative words reap negative harvests/positive words reap positive harvests)

Are the words you speak to others intended to make them feel better or worse?

Are the words that you speak spirit and life, like those of Jesus (John 6:63), or

Are you speaking and sowing words of flesh, failure and death (Galatians 6:8)?

In what areas do you need improvement?

What negative words do you need to stop speaking to or about others?

What negative words do you need to stop speaking about yourself?

What positive words of blessing and truth do you need to start speaking about yourself and to others?

Chapter Seven:

The Gift of Hearing

The Ears of the Face

The ears are placed on either side of the face. They are for our hearing. They are one of the gates wherein information is received and then processed internally, resulting in a possible external response through the face or other parts of the body.

Often we hear with our ears, but we are not really listening. We just pick up the sound of the words and hear, but we are not really listening. When we do not "listen" to what we hear, we cannot gain knowledge and understanding.

We can hear and call ourselves listening, yet not understand the meaning of what we just heard. How many times have you said to someone or vice versa, "Oh I heard you, but I thought you meant thus and so." Often the response of the sender might be "How could you think I meant that?" This is what you call "hearing, without understanding the meaning of what you heard."

Hearing and Understanding the Voice/Sound

Many of us long to "hear" the voice of the Lord. Could it be that He *is* speaking, but we have not learned how to listen? Jesus said, "My sheep know my voice and a stranger they will not follow." The question is have we listened to the voice of the Shepherd, such that we "know" His voice when we hear it? Are our ears as attentive to His voice, as He is to ours? When we hear His voice, do we understand the meaning of His voice?

When the Lord asked Adam in Genesis 3:8-10, "Where are you?" do you really think the Lord did not know where he was? Often, when God asks us a question, it is not because He does not know the answer, but instead his questions gives us an opportunity to examine who, what and where we are and how we got there.

Yes, "Adam, where are you?" was simply the Lord's way of revealing to Adam where he (Adam) really was. It is very interesting that Adam did not ever answer the question physically, e.g., "I'm behind the tree," but rather, he answered it mentally, emotionally and spiritually.

Adam said to the Lord, "I heard your voice and I was afraid." His reply revealed where he was mentally and emotionally. "I heard your voice and I felt fear, because I was naked; (I was exposed; my darkness was revealed in the light)." Adam goes on the say, "and I hid myself." This response revealed where Adam was spiritually. Who and what was Adam hiding from? From the very Voice and Presence of God.

The Lord already knew where Adam was, physically, mentally, emotionally and spiritually, but He wanted Adam to acknowledge and recognize it for himself.

The Voice of the Lord (The Word of God) is truth and will always bring conviction upon those that "have an EAR to hear what the Spirit of God is saying/meaning."

The Presence of God will sometimes cause us to want to run and hide, because His Presence reveals the darkness in our lives. Our natural response to being naked, discovered or exposed, is to run and hide. What we **should** do, is humble ourselves, own our own garbage, ask for forgiveness and be cleansed from all unrighteousness (I John 1:9).

Whenever we desire to hide from the Lord, even though He knows the truth, we will also be tempted to blame someone other than ourselves. When the Lord asked Adam in Gen. 3:11, "Have you eaten of the tree which I commanded you that you should not eat?" Adam quickly transferred the blame not only to the woman, but first and foremost to God Himself. Adam's response was "The woman **YOU** gave to be with me, **SHE** gave me of the tree and I did eat."

What was Adam saying to the Lord? "God, it is **Your** fault that I sinned and fell short of your glory. It is **Your** fault because, **You** made this woman and then gave her to me. If **You** had not made her, this would never have happened."

How often do we feel and believe that same lie? How many times do we blame others for our failures, instead of admitting that we had an alternative choice? How many times, if we would tell ourselves the truth, have we blamed God Himself, for the situations that we have had to face in our lives, when in fact, most of them were the result of failure to obey the word of God, and acknowledge and repent of our own sins?

How often, have we or do we still "justify" our unrighteous or unkind thoughts and deeds, by pointing the finger at someone other than ourselves? Do you ever say or feel something like this? "If they had not said or done this or that, then I would not have said or done this or that." How about this one. "She, he, or they started it, and I'm just finishing it," or "I forgive so and so, but I will never ever forget it." It is time for us to not only hear, but understand the meaning of the voice that speaks to us. It is time to really develop a *listening* ear.

The "Listening" Ear

The book of Revelations contains multiple verses that say, "He that hath an ear, let him hear what the Spirit is saying unto the churches." (Rev 2:7, 11, 17, 29; 3:6, 13)

This new testament word "hear" comes from the Greek word "Akono" and it means; to understand; to hear with the ear of the mind. In this sense it means not just to hear a sound, or a voice, but to understand the meaning of the sound or voice.

> We will never enter into this kind of "hearing" until we have learned to listen with the ear of the mind and the ear of understanding, that comes from the Spirit of the Lord.

There is something called "active listening," whereby you feed back to a person, what you understood them to say and at the same time express your understanding of what they actually meant.

Active Listening feedback goes something like this:

The person that is listening says to the one that was speaking:

"If I am hearing you correctly, you are saying thus and so. If I'm understanding you correctly, this is what you mean?" This then allows the person who was speaking, to determine, if you have understood what they said and meant.

What would happen, if we practiced active listening when it comes to the voice/word of God? If we said, "Lord, If I'm **hearing you** correctly, you are saying thus and so. If I understand what I am hearing, does this mean, thus and so in my life?" "Lord, are you saying I should think, speak or do this or I shouldn't think speak or do that? Lord, is this what you meant when you said … in your word?

I believe that when we let the Lord know we are actively "listening," we will be able to hear, with the "ear of the mind." God will then open up the *eyes* of our understanding and enlighten us, as to the meaning of His Voice.

A listening ear will only come to those who are willing to admit that sometimes they 1) don't hear at all; 2) hear, but are not really listening; or 3) hear, but not with the ear of the mind/understanding.

If we are not willing to at least acknowledge our need to develop an ear that really hears, then we probably will never hear with the "ear of the mind."

The Inner Ear

There is a phrase that most of us have heard, that says, "the problem with most people lies between their two ears," meaning our mind. There is a lot of truth to this. However, I submit for your consideration, that the mind just might be confused because we have not developed an ear that actually "hears the voice and understands the meaning of the voice."

The physical ear, consists of an outer and inner ear. Think of the outer ear as the ear that hears the sound or voice and think of the inner ear as that part that "understands the meaning" of the sound or voice. We must begin to hear with this inner ear and not just the outer ear. There is a phrase called turning a "deaf" ear, which can be thought of as the inner ear, refusing to receive the sound or voice, that is coming through the outer ear.

The inner ear says, "I am deaf, I do not want to hear, see, understand or take heed. I already know all I need or want to know, so I will turn away so that I cannot hear. I will respond as though I am deaf." Are you aware, when you are turning a deaf ear naturally and/or spiritually? If you pay attention, you will begin to recognize your own body language. Usually the head, "the face," actually turns to the left or the right with a slight jerk, as if to say, "Talk to the hand, cause the inner ear refuses to hear and understand." The eyes may even roll around and close. I assure you, a **deaf ear** is never in a position to send or receive a blessing.

Questions/Reflections:

1. Do you believe you have an ear that "hears?" Explain your answer.

2. Could your listening skills be improved? If so, how?

3. Do you often interrupt while others are talking? If so, why?

4. When are you most likely to turn a "deaf" ear and to whom?

5. Are you easy to be "entreated," approached or talked to?

6. What steps do you need to take, to have a better ear to hear?

7. Have you learned how to listen to the "body language" of others?

8. Are you aware of your own body language? Do you need improvement?

Chapter Eight:

Understanding
<u>Grace, Mercy and Repentance</u>

<u>Invoking the LORD'S Blessing</u>

The blessing recorded in Numbers 6:22- 27, teaches us what God Himself considers a blessing. He indicated, there was a specific way His chosen people, the Israelites, were to be blessed. First of all, the blessing was to be spoken.

God said "say to them," thus and so. This lets us know that in order to bless someone, you need to "say" it. Not just smile or express it in some other way, but "say it." It is the words we speak that cause the blessing to come to pass.

So the LORD told Moses the exact words for Aaron and his sons to say, which would invoke the LORD's blessing upon His children. He said, "Say to them," "The LORD bless you, watch guard and keep you." This word **bless,** in the Hebrew is Barak (baw-rak'), which means, for God to bless in such a way that you will personally benefit. Barak means, when God initiates a blessing upon you, just because **He has decided to do it**, though you may not deserve it.

It is God loving you, **on purpose**, regardless of your works, plus or minus. It is God bestowing His blessing on the just and the unjust. It is God loving you unconditionally, in spite of everything He knows about you. I call this "the agape, on purpose" blessing of the LORD upon you, which **no one can curse.**

This Aaronic blessing, requests that the LORD not only bless you, but watch guard over you and keep you (Numbers 6:24).

What do you need to be guarded and kept from? From the purpose of the thief, the enemy of our soul, who came to steal, kill and destroy. This blessing of the LORD, overrides the purposes of the evil one and gives us life, eternal God life and that more abundantly. (John 10:10) Let's look at the blessings of Grace and Mercy, that is imparted from the LORD to us through His Face.

The Face of Grace

The spoken blessing continues: "The LORD make His face to shine upon and enlighten you and be gracious (kind, merciful, and giving favor) to you." (Numbers 6:25, Amplified)

This verse reveals to us the very intent that God had, when He created our face in His own image. God considers it a blessing when His face shines upon us and enlightens us, opening up our understanding and imparting revelation to us. He considers it a blessing when we are the recipient and benefactor of His grace (unmerited, undeserved favor and mercy). He made us in His image and likeness and we were created to be like Him, full of grace and truth. (John 1:14)

The purpose of our face then, is to be to someone else, what God's Face is to us. In other words, **your face was created to shine upon someone else's face and bless them, by allowing the light of God within you to shine through you,**

so that someone else, may behold the glory of the Lord when they look upon our face. Your face was made to shine the light of God, upon every dark and hopeless area of their life, revealed by the look on their face. Your face was made to impart grace (unmerited, undeserved favor) to others. Grace, is giving and imparting to others, what they have **not** worked for and do not deserve. This is called "favor."

Have you ever heard the phrase "Give me grace?" I was amazed the first time I heard someone say this. This request came from a leader who was chairing a meeting. She was tired, not feeling up to par and was not as prepared as she would have liked to have been, for the particular item on the agenda. She simply asked "Would you give me grace this morning?" Meaning, do you have enough love in your heart, to give me grace and not criticize or judge my faults? Will you give me your understanding and be willing to hold up my arms, while I "go through?" "Will you extend love and even forgiveness, if today I happen not to meet the standards you have set for me? If I happen to breach a contract that **you** made concerning me, that I never signed?" **"Will You, Give Me Grace?"**

Of course, she did not say all that I have written, but simply asked for grace. May I just tell you, that this was a reminder to me, that God, is not the only one who can impart grace to others. We can and are to give grace, willingly, lovingly and in abundance to those that need it, even if they don't ask for it. It came to me, that when I refrain from criticizing, judging, or being impatient or unkind when others perform less than 100%, that in fact, I am "giving them grace." What a beautiful revelation! We **can all** be like the Lord, if we try! We can all give grace to others and be loving and kind, through our face.

The Grace Test

1. Do you find it difficult to give grace to others? If so, why?

2. In the past year, have you personally been the object of someone else's grace, including the Lord? What was it concerning?

3. Does your face reflect the blessing of graciousness to your loved ones? To your friends? To others?

4. Does your face indicate that you are approachable and full of grace and that you are ready to impart the blessing of grace and kindness to those that need it? OR Does your face reflect, "Don't even try it!"

5. List 1-2 changes that may need to be made in your heart, and soul (mind, emotions, and will), so you can extend more grace to others through your face.

6. Are you willing to develop and monitor a progress plan on extending grace to others, using the word of God as your guide and encourager?

7. Monitor your progress with a friend and the Holy Spirit.

The Face of Mercy

"Oh give thanks unto the Lord for He is good, for His mercy endures forever (Psalm 118:1)."

Your face was also made to extend mercy, which means **not** imparting to others what they **really do** deserve. (Blessed are the merciful, for they shall receive mercy, Matthew 5:7). This verse is one of the greatest incentives in the Bible, (extending mercy to the guilty), because it promises that when you are guilty of wrongdoing, you too will receive mercy, from both God and man.

> Mercy, is one of the attributes of God. The greatest power in being a God, is not the power to create, control or destroy life, but the power to extend abundant mercy, so that others might live and not die; So that others may receive more than one chance or opportunity to fulfill their foreordained destiny.

Many have said that God is the God of the second chance. I am certain you will agree, that He is the God of countless chances and opportunities to know Him, walk upright before Him and receive our inheritance in Him. He not only gives us another chance, He woos us by giving us incentives to repent. If God's incentives were money, we would all be financially secure.

Incentives – God's Strategy For Repentance

> God's never ending mercy is one of His many attributes. It is His Goodness. Scripture teaches us that "His goodness causes us to repent." The express purpose of God's mercy is to cause us to change our thoughts and subsequent actions/ deeds. One of the ways He has chosen to do this, is through incentives. Does God give us incentives to do right? Yes, because right actions release God to bless you and blessing you brings Him pleasure.

The scriptures are full of incentives, to allow righteousness to rule and reign in our hearts. Does not God understand parenting better than we do? Often we hear that you should not "bribe" your children or give incentives to get them to do the right thing. I do not fully agree with this thinking. First of all bribery and incentives are two different things. Bribery is deceitful and is therefore not of the Lord, while the word of the Lord is loaded with incentives to help us and even encourage us to make a decision for righteousness. I wonder why?

It is so interesting to discover in the word of God, that even when the Lord was angry with His people, He still gave them incentives to repent, obey and walk in righteousness. He uses the If, then, else or the "Because you disobeyed…, then I'm going to… BUT if you repent…then I will bless you," instead of passing judgment on you." May I just say, that the bible is full of incentives to encourage us to live and not die. Many examples are in the book of Revelations.

The letters to the seven churches in the book of Revelations Chapters 2 through Chapter 3:22, are full of incentives. I love the way the Lord gives performance evaluations. He always tells first what we have done that has pleased Him. Then He lets us know what He has against us. (Do you ever want the Lord to be against you?) Thank God for Jesus, that the evaluation does not end there, but instead gives an incentive to repent (change your mind, attitude, thoughts and actions), and overcome the spirit of disobedience, (self-governing, self -indulgence, self-righteousness, self-love, unbelief and such like). Just look at the following incentives the Lord spoke to the churches. He is speaking the same thing to you, because *you* are the church.

The letters to the seven churches provide incentives, by listing the rewards that will be bestowed upon those who are willing to change and overcome. Some will "eat from the tree of life, which is in the midst of the Paradise of God." Others, will receive "the crown of life," and others "hidden manna and a new name on a white stone."

Still others, will "rule over the nations and receive the morning star" and others will be "clothed in white garments and honored before the Father."

Some will become "pillars in the temple of God and receive a new name" and others will "be granted the blessing of sitting with Jesus on His Throne," because they **overcame as He did.** How many more incentives do we need, to soften our hard hearts?

How much more does the Lord have to promise us, to get us to change? What else does He have to do, to get us to believe that He has thoughts and plans of good and not evil for our future (Jeremiah 29:11)? These are questions you must ask yourself, meditate on and decide to consider your own ways toward the Lord, ourselves and others.

It would be a step in the right direction if we took lessons from the book of Revelations, when we evaluate someone face to face. In summary, we should follow the model given in Revelations. Affirm, encourage and validate first, then in truth and love, correct and/or rebuke. Lastly, give incentives, by indicating the reward that will come, if they are willing to repent (change their mind). This is how the Holy Spirit evaluates us, as He continues to perform a good work in us, until the day of Jesus Christ (Philippians 1:6).

The Face of Conviction vs. Condemnation

The Holy Spirit brings "conviction" not "condemnation" (John 16:8). We must understand the difference between these two methods of evaluation and judgment. The word of God encourages us not to judge, but if we do, be careful to use righteous judgment (Matthew 7:1-2). It is not only speaking of correct judgment, but also means we must not condemn before we convict. What is He really saying? ***To "convict" means "to convince of error, with a kindly intent towards corrective action,"*** which simply says to someone, "I am bringing this to your attention so you can repent, change your action, go another direction, and/or do something different." Conviction doesn't leave you hanging in the air trying to figure out what to do, but constructive criticism/conviction will also suggest what you need to do or consider, in order to bring about the desired results.

> ***Condemnation on the other hand, does not afford any opportunity for corrective action, as the word actually means, "to sentence to doom or death."***

Condemnation is the end of the line. It is a final judgment with no more time or space to repent. It is the end...death. Your name is blotted out of the Lamb's Book of Life. To be spiritually condemned, means eternal separation from God and everlasting life forever. It is not the Holy Spirit of God that condemns us, but the enemy of our souls who condemns us, although he did not die for us (Romans 8:34). Christ died for us and as such, is the only one that has the power and authority to condemn us. Yet, He convicts us instead. He convinces us of our errors with a kindly intent towards corrective action. He alone has the keys of hell and of death. Yet, He came that we might have/choose life.

The strategy of the enemy, is to get us to listen to his voice of condemnation, which when we agree with him, causes us to condemn ourselves.

Do you understand that condemnation by the enemy, others and even yourself does not bring repentance? In fact it actually sets sin on fire. Condemnation inflames sin and causes it to become worse. It is the loving "conviction" of the Holy Spirit of God, the abundant goodness, mercy and grace of God, that empowers us, enlightens and strengthens us, so we CAN know the truth and repent.

Scripture tells us, that "Godly sorrow brings forth repentance," but another scripture says, "His goodness causes us to repent." Both, of course, are true but wouldn't it be wonderful if we would allow His goodness to change our minds, thoughts, emotions and deeds?

Why must we, more often than not, have to experience sorrow, pain, heartache, despair, and such before we say "yes" to the will of the Lord? When we begin to seek the face of the Lord so we can understand and receive the Aaronic blessing for our lives, then we will allow His goodness to cause us to repent and change.

Questions/Reflections:

1. When someone looks into your face, what do they see?

2. Does your face shine light, hope, joy, and revelation?

3. Does your face impart grace and mercy to others?

4. Does your face say to others, I am approachable and a safe place for you? I really care about what you are going through?

5. Can you identify times when you have deliberately been merciful and kind?

Chapter Nine:

Let's Face It

The Face of Approval and Peace

The Aaronic blessing continues: (Numbers 6:26)

"The Lord lift up His (approving) countenance upon you and give you peace (tranquility of heart and life continually)." (Amplified)

When the countenance of someone's face is one of approval towards us, it gives us peace in our heart and adds to our life. So much of our life is spent seeking approval from loved ones, friends, authority and even people we do not know or have relationship with. The latter group is called "They." How often have you made an important even life changing decision, based on what "they" may or may not think, say or do? Yes, we tend to hunger, seek after and need the approval of men.

Oh what joy would come into our hearts and lives, if we had as strong a desire to obtain approval from the one who should matter to us the most, i.e., the approval of Almighty God.

When others look upon your countenance, do they see approval or dis-approval? Are you aware, that your face was actually made to change the countenance on someone else's face in a positive way? From darkness to light. From depression to hope. From death to life. From rejection and disapproval to acceptance and approval?

In other words, your face was made to put a smile on every sad face you encounter. Your face was created to impart comfort and joy wherever there is mourning and sorrow. To impart hope, where there is none. The world is in great need of hope, not just for today but for tomorrow. We are living in an hour where people, even the people of God, are in need of encouragement and a reason to get up the next day.

In my opinion, many suicides are committed by people that simply want to go to sleep and escape for just a day or two. They simply can't cope with the next 24 – 48 hours. I believe this with all my heart, as I have observed and experienced life's many trials, tribulations, temptations and intimidation's. What a difference 24-48 little hours can make in every situation and circumstance. If we could just let those contemplating suicide go somewhere and sleep for a few days, I believe when they woke up they would feel totally different.

Just think of your own difficult experiences. It is amazing, how differently you thought and felt about them 24-48 hours later. The times when you *felt* you could not go any further; you could not face the future; you had no reason to live; no one cared whether you lived or died; when your freedom was threatened; no finances, no friends...whatever, no matter how bleak things looked, 24-48 hours later, you were able to cope just a little better.

Your face can give someone that really needs it, that approval, peace and rest.

You may be thinking, My face? Yes, your face, with all of its possible flaws. Yet, your face was made by

God Himself to impart the blessing of approval and peace, to others. The faces of others were made especially for **you** to receive the same blessing from them.

To impart to others and receive from others, the blessing of approval, support, unity, validation, joy, understanding, safety, mercy, peace and grace was and still is, God's original intent and purpose for your face and mine.

A High Price for Peace

When anyone lifts up their countenance upon us and imparts to us peace, it physically causes our heart to become tranquil, which in turn causes circulation to flow properly, providing life (blood/oxygen) to every part of our body.

Have you ever experienced a warmth go through your body, especially your face, when someone looks at you in a peaceful accepting way? Not in an invasive or violating or intimidating way, but with warm approval or admiration? Peace is one of the most needful things your face can impart to another person.

One of the words for peace in Hebrew is called "Shalom." Shalom, comes from the root word "Shalam," which means to be complete, perfect and full.

Shalom is more detailed and means:

Completeness, wholeness, peace, health, welfare, safety, soundness, tranquility, prosperity, perfectness, fullness, rest, harmony; the absence of agitation and discord.

Shalom, is said to even be much more than the absence of war, agitation and conflict, it is the wholeness that the entire world seeks.

Note: This definition and explanation was taken from the Spirit Filled Life Bible, Word Wealth for Shalom in the book of Nahum 1:15.

Shalom is the same word used in Isaiah 53:5:

"But He was wounded for our transgressions, He was bruised for our iniquities; the ***chastisement*** *for our* ***peace*** *was upon Him and by His stripes we are healed.*"

Jesus Christ of Nazareth was chastised, so that you and I could receive peace (Shalom) and all of the many things that are included in Shalom.

The price for Shalom has already been paid. Shalom comes to us through the New Covenant, established on the Cross, through the broken Body and shed Blood of Jesus Christ.

Shalom, can be imparted to others through "your face," and received from others through their face, which then becomes "the place of blessing" for us.

Questions/Reflections:

What part(s) of Shalom have you received from the face of another? In what area has it helped you?

What part(s) of Shalom do you need from others?

What part(s) of Shalom are you willing to impart to others through your face?

Meditate on the truth that Jesus was chastised so you could have the fullness of Shalom operating in your life. Is this truth activated in your life?

Look up other scriptures with the words that are included in Shalom. Receive Shalom for yourself. Pray for Shalom in the lives of others.

Face Cleansing Time:

Reflect on those times when you have NOT imparted Shalom to someone.

Ask for forgiveness from the Lord. Now forgive yourself. If applicable, ask the person to forgive you, for missing your opportunity to impart Shalom to them when they needed it most. (Be wise about this.)

If the person is not aware of your fault or attitude towards them, it may be wise to keep it between you and the Lord, rather than dump this on them and then they may have a hard time understanding and getting over it.)

Make a decision to change your mind and handle things differently in the future. (Repentance equals a changed mind/direction/action)

Practice imparting one or more characteristics of Shalom to someone everyday. (Look for opportunities. They are all around you.)

Keys to Relationship/Intimacy

God created your face, as the initial place of relationship and intimacy. The face is the first sight where love or hate is determined, sometimes at first glance. The face serves as the beginning or end of possibilities for relationship and intimacy. How many times have you felt a slap in the face just by the countenance on someone else's face? How often have you felt that someone was "sizing you up and down" by the look on their faces?

Often broken relationships come from a lack of looking at or into the face of the one we have relationship with. It has been said that the *eyes are*

the windows to the soul, (intellect, emotions, will/
desires).

When you try to build a relationship without
connecting to the soul of a person, it will only be a
superficial relationship and not a relationship of the
heart.

Relationship is the key to the heart and truth. True
relationship always reveals what is hidden deep in
the recesses of our hearts.

Superficial relationships often appear to be successful,
simply because the substance of the relationship is
not one deep in the heart. When we keep others at
arms length and never allow anyone to invade our
intimate zone, our relationships will never be heart
to heart revealing ones.

Many relationships are of the performance type,
rather than the heart type. In other words, the
relationship is built on what one "does," rather than
who one **is.** Performance only proves what you can
do, but true relationship invades your intimate zone
and reveals what is really in your heart or rather, who
you really are underneath all your various masks.

Relationship then, is meant to show you who you
are at a given point in your life, so you can make the
necessary adjustments or changes in order to grow
and fulfill the destiny God intended for you. All of
this is dependent on your willingness to accept and
admit the possibility, how ever so slight, of yourself
being imperfect. (Tongue in cheek)

For many years, I believed I had good relationships
with everyone. I often said with pride, "I can get along
with anyone, even those that others cannot handle."
I used to love to make friends with someone that
no one else liked or could not develop a friendship

with. I always felt I had excellent interpersonal skills and an insight into the needs of others. It was years before I was able to understand true relationship and discover the many flaws to my thinking and philosophy. What I considered for years to be relationship, was not relationship at all, but rather was more of a performance oriented acquaintance with others.

I confused my ability to "get the job done" and "getting along with people" with relationship. I have since changed my thinking and as a result, I believe I have become a better person and leader, willing to take the risk of allowing someone to enter into my intimate zone and "know" me.

I confused my ability to get others to work, serve, participate and act, with relationship from the heart.

I began to realize in recent years, why I had supposedly good relationship with almost everyone. The reason being was because I had my own set of guidelines for a successful relationship. These guidelines were my own philosophy based on years of living and learning, failing and succeeding. My built-in guidelines included such philosophies as:

"Live and let live. Give others their space."

"Don't ask people their **business** and keep them out of yours."

"Do not pry or ask someone for their personal information, such as their salary, amount of savings, financial plans, financial ability, and plans for their future. Stay out of your friend's relationship and family conflicts. Keep your opinions to yourself." This is outer court relationship and is not heart to heart. You will never intimately know a person or even what is in your heart, if you use this philosophy with regard to friendships.

The Face of Leadership

In 1996 I was privileged to become one of the Board of Directors of Aglow International and also a Director of the Aglow U.S. National Board. During my tenure, sitting under the leadership of Jane Hansen, President and CEO of Aglow International, I have learned much more about true relationship and Apostolic leadership.

I have come away from annual board meetings, totally changed and humbled by the openness, honesty, humility and love of this leader among leaders, chosen by God as an Apostle, an Esther and a Mother of Israel to the Nations of the world. I have learned the price one must be willing to pay, in order to have a heart to heart relationship with God and man.

True heart relationships require faith, hope and love. Mature relationship with God and man only comes as you are willing to die. Die? Yes, die. Die to yourself, even your spiritual dreams and visions. Die, to your position in the Lord. Die, to the timing of when the prophetic words of the Lord concerning you will come to pass. Die, to misunderstandings. Die, to the fiery darts that came, not from those who are your enemies, but rather those who broke bread with you at your table. Die, to the right to "control" others because you are the leader. Die, die, die.

I do not recall who first taught this, but I have learned that dying also means, we must be willing to offer ourselves, on the Altar of the Lord. Why? So that after you have been melted and your flesh burnt up by the fire of His Spirit, God can then, out of the ashes, mold and make you after His will. Then, you will truly be a vessel of honor, fit for His use. You will have been refined in the fire.

You may be called to one of the five-fold ministries, Apostle, Prophet, Evangelist, Pastor, Teacher, but the question is, are you willing to become a true follower of Christ, and die, in order to become a leader like the Lord?

Have you ever been willing to "wait" to implement something that you know, that "God said," just because the leaders that you are in relationship with do not all agree? Have you ever been willing to "die" to what you believe is the voice of God, until He releases the grace that is necessary for the vision to succeed? (Grace in this case, being unity and acceptance and understanding of those that will be charged to "run" with the vision).

There is so much to learn about relationship and the heart. Oh, what a revelation when you discover that much of our concerns in our natural relationships are either all, or mostly all, about us. This same attitude, if not changed, crosses over into our spiritual relationship with the Lord. Some of our relationships are not heart to heart, but network to network, stepping stone to stepping stone, performance to performance, about me to more about me.

What would happen, if we would stop "helping God" reveal us to the world? What would happen, if we stopped trying to out-preach, out-teach, out-dance, out-sing, out-do one another, so we could get "top-billing" as the Man or Woman of the Hour? What would happen if we would allow our flesh to die?

On the other hand, what would happen, if we just accepted the truth and stopped living in false humility? The truth being, that we all have **something** to contribute to this world. **Something** that this world needs. That **something** is deep on the inside of every person. Each of us, has a deep down, even hidden desire to bring forth or birth the **something** we are to contribute to the world. Competition, rivalry, envy and jealousy is born, due to fear, doubt and unbelief, that we don't have anything to contribute or impart to others. Confidence in God, rather than ability and reliance on self, is what motivates and builds true relationships. God desires that whatever we bring forth would be known as a "Holy Thing." God's word encourages all of us, and especially His Leaders to "Be Holy for I am Holy."

I recall when Jane Hansen, Aglow International President and CEO spoke in 1998 at the Aglow Annual Conference. Her message was on Holiness and she gave one of the definitions of Holiness. She said, "holiness is honesty." When she spoke these words, the revelation of the truth, went through my entire body, as I realized Holiness is not just "doing Holy things," but it means to **become** a Holy being. Truth on the inward parts, is what the Lord desires and requires. Honesty equals openness and transparency, nothing hidden, no deceit.

The Lord had also given me, as a speaker for that same conference, that Holiness, is "the absence of darkness." Holiness is light, being transparent, nothing hidden, no manipulation, nothing impure. This then, is how you can become a leader after God's own heart. A leader, who has discovered how to walk in true holiness before the Lord. A Leader, who has studied to show yourself approved unto God. A person that does not need to be ashamed of the Gospel of Jesus Christ. One who is able to rightly divide the Word of Truth. If you endeavor to be(come) a person whose objective is to be open and honest, the Lord will use your life for His Glory and call you into leadership.

The Face of
Encouragement and Correction

There is much weariness, discouragement, despair and hopelessness in this world. This is why, your face and mine were fashioned by God to impart strength, hope and encouragement to those who are alone, weary and fearful, so they would not faint, but instead would press on and overcome "until the end."

Revelation 2:7 teaches us, that those who overcome, will eat from the tree of life in the midst of the Paradise of God.

Revelation 2:10,11 teaches us, that those who do not grow weary, but are faithful until death, will receive "a crown of life" and will not be hurt by the second death. Revelation 2:17 teaches us, that those who overcome, will be given hidden manna to eat and a white stone with a new name written, which know one knows except the one who gives it. Revelation 2:26; 3:5, 12 and 21 all contain incentives to bring about repentance and they also include the rewards that will be bestowed on those who are willing to obey.

What a loving, kind, long-suffering, merciful God! What a wonderful Savior, Counselor and Friend! Again, in Revelations, Chapters Two and Three, the Lord tells the Churches (The Body of Christ), four basic things:

1) What they were doing that was good; 2) What they were doing that was not good; 3) What would happen if they did not repent and lastly; 4) The

incentive or reward that would be theirs, if they chose to obey and repent.

This is what I love about the Lord: He always corrects His people before it is too late. If we would just be willing to obey and heed his voice, on the very day we hear his voice, we would put ourselves in a position for His goodness and mercy to continue to follow us all the days of our life. Remember, God equates His goodness with His Glory.

Questions/Reflections

1. When others are weary, discouraged and hopeless, are you impatient with them?

2. When you give counsel, are you too quick to tell them how to solve their problems, or are you willing to listen and "hear" their heart first?

   Do you begin with what the person has done right or do you start right in telling them what they have not done and need to do?

3. Do you indicate what was incorrect and why? Do you give incentives for change and correction? Do you consider giving early warning counsel or do you wait until it is almost too late for change and correction?

4. When they are ready to give up, are you willing to help them and hold up their arms until they overcome?

5. What does your face impart to them, as they reveal their problems to you?

   Does your face impart strength, hope or courage? Does it say, "Well, what did you expect? You should have known better? Why are you telling me at this late date?" OR,

6. Does your face say what Jesus said? "I will never leave you nor forsake you." Or does your countenance say, "I will sit this one out with you? You will not have to bear this burden alone?"

Chapter Ten:

The Name, Face and Suffering of God

His Name Invokes His Blessing

"So they (the priests), shall put My name
on the children of Israel and I will bless
them."(Numbers 6:27)

This last verse of what is known as the Aaronic
blessing (Numbers 6:27), reveals to us what happens
when we allow our face to become a blessing to
someone else in the ways described in Numbers
6:22-26: Let's review them:

The Lord spoke first to Moses saying:

"Speak to Aaron *(the High Priest)* and his sons
(the priests) saying:

"This is the way you are to **bless** *(italics mine)* the
children of Israel. **Say** to them: *(in other words
this blessing is to be spoken through your
face/mouth.)*"" (Numbers 6:23)

"The LORD bless you and keep you; (Numbers
6:24)

The LORD make His face shine upon you, And be
gracious to you; (Numbers 6:24-25)

The LORD lift up His countenance upon you and
give you peace." (Numbers 6:26)

"So they *(the priests)* shall put My name on the children of Israel, and I will bless them." (Numbers 6:27)

These verses show us the heart of God and His desire to teach us how we can cause the people to be blessed by Him. He has given to all of us, the exact words to speak into and over His children. He then reveals how they are actually going to receive the blessing (verse 27). When we speak what is known as "The Aaronic Blessing" over the children of God, we figuratively place the Name of the Lord upon them. When the Lord sees His Name upon His children, He then fulfills His promise to bless them. If you are a child of God, then this blessing is yours to receive and also impart to others.

Will you choose to believe that the Lord made you in His image and His likeness and He desires that you do with your face, what He delights in doing?

Will you believe that *you* can actually cause someone to receive the blessings of the LORD, when you pronounce this blessing upon them from your heart?

Consider this. God desires that our faces shine on others and bless them, speaking the very words that will cause the Lord to look upon them and bless them too.

The LORD delights in blessing people. He blesses us, even when we do not deserve it. He forgave our sins long before we ever committed them. That is what forgiveness really means. Consider this definition of forgive: To forgive, means to (pre) give, to give ahead of time. To give prior to the offense.

> **If we would be willing to walk in the spirit of forgiveness, choosing to forgive others in advance of their transgressions against us, our lives would totally be changed and enriched. We would begin to understand the cross.**

His Face Imparts the Blessing

In Exodus Chapter 33:18,19, Moses asks the LORD "Please show me Your glory." **The Lord's response was "I will make all MY goodness pass before you, and I will proclaim the name of the Lord before you. I will be gracious to whom I will be gracious, and I will have compassion on whom I will have compassion." But He said, "You cannot see MY face; for no man shall see Me and live."**

Many people have indicated that they have seen the Face of the Lord in dreams and visions.

In the book of Revelations 1:13-17, the Apostle John describes the face of God: ..**One like the Son of Man, clothed with a garment down to the feet and girded about the chest with a golden band. His head and hair were white like wool, as white as snow, and His eyes like a flame of fire;**

His feet were like fine brass, as if refined in a furnace, and His voice as the sound of many waters. He had in His right hand seven stars, out of His mouth went a sharp two-edged sword, and His countenance was like the sun shining in its strength.

And when I saw Him, I fell at His feet as dead. But He laid His right hand on me saying to

me, "Do not be afraid; I am the First and the Last. I am He who lives, and was dead, and behold, I am alive forevermore. Amen. And I have the keys of Hades and of Death."

For years, I have longed to see the Face of Jesus in a dream or vision. I have imagined that His Face would be very strong and powerful, yet gentle and glorious, awesome to behold, and in other words, just plain beautiful.

There has been controversy over the face of Jesus, with regard to the pictures we see of Christ in this century. Some say He did not look like the soft mild face we see. Others have said He had very strong features. Isaiah 53:2 states: "He has no form nor comeliness; and when we see Him, There is no beauty that we should desire Him." Some say His skin was fair, still others say it was dark, even black.

It has never concerned me as to what color the skin of Jesus was, because as we all know, skin is only a body suit for this atmosphere. Skin cannot go through doors, neither can it enter into Heaven. We will all be resurrected with a glorified body. God does not have a skin color people. Rise and be healed!

My longing to see the Face of Jesus continued to increase, as I heard others tell of visions they had of seeing His body and His feet. I too wanted to behold His glory and look into His eyes of love. For years, I stayed at the feet of Jesus, because I could not bear to look up because of shame. (The face of shame always looks down.)

A few years ago, I was invited to speak at a women's retreat. During praise and worship they sang "Open the eyes of my heart Lord, I want to see you." As the words were repeated over and over, "I want to see you," I was weeping and worshipping the Lord. In my spirit, I heard a small voice say, "Do you really want to see me?" I responded, "Yes Lord, I really want to see you." I then heard this small voice say, "Then open your eyes."

When I opened my eyes, I saw the faces of all the people who had come to the retreat. The small voice within said…."Herein is my face. Look for me in the people. Open the eyes of your heart, and you will see me in them. That which you desire to do for me, do for them. Such as I have given to you, give to them. Things I have revealed to you, reveal to them. The love you desire to pour out on me, pour out on them and you will be pouring it out on me. What you do unto others, you are doing unto me."

When we grasp this truth, it will enhance our relationships and cause them to be built on truth and intimacy. We will begin to look for God in every face, even those faces that try to intimidate us and make us afraid. Perfect love, God's love, casts out fear.

The face that gives what it longs for first, is the face that will receive that which they have hungered for. It is written, give and you shall receive. Sow and you shall reap.

His Suffering Paid for the Blessing

In March of 2004, after over 20 years of not attending movie theaters, while at Aglow International Board of Director meetings in Seattle, Washington, we went to see the movie, The Passion of the Christ. It had been out for a few weeks already and something was stirring inside of me to go. It was as though I needed to go, as though something new would be revealed to me.

114

When I left the Theater, I felt as though after all these years my desire to see the Face of the Lord had been fulfilled. I believe I truly saw the Face of the Lord.

Not the face that I imagined, but nevertheless The Face of God. The Face described in the Book of Isaiah, Chapter 52 and 53.

Isaiah 52:13-14 states: Behold, my Servant shall deal prudently; He shall be exalted and extolled and be very high. Just as many were astonished at you, So His visage (appearance) was marred more than any man, and His form more than the sons of men.

Isaiah 53:3-5 states: He is despised and rejected by men. A Man of sorrows and acquainted with grief. And we hid as it were, our faces from Him; He was despised and we did not esteem Him.

Surely He has borne our griefs And carried our sorrows; Yet we esteemed Him stricken, Smitten by God, and afflicted. But He was wounded for our transgressions. He was bruised for our iniquities; the chastisement for our peace was upon Him, And by His stripes we are healed.

These scriptures reveal the Face of God. The Face, that was marred beyond recognition. The Face, that was rejected despised and not esteemed. The Face, of Love, Compassion and Suffering. The Face that says…I Love, I give, and I forgive **unconditionally**. The Face that says, you so ravish my heart, that I will lay down my life for you (Song of Songs 4:9). I will drink of the bitter cup for the sake of the purposes and plans of God my Father for this world.

Yes, you and I have been made in the image and likeness of God, and His desire is that we would be imitators of Him. We were not only created to represent Him, but to re-present to others, all that He was on this earth and all that He still is.

Your face and mine should be the "place of blessing" to those people that behold us and come near to us. Once we become fully aware of our ability to bless others through the messages sent from/through our face, we too will be a recipient of the blessings of the Lord that make rich and adds no sorrow.

Chapter Eleven:

Face-to-Face Exercise

Imparting The Spoken Aaronic Blessing

This exercise has purposely been made the last Chapter. It is my hope that the entire book would be read before doing this face to face exercise. The reason being that you the reader would have the full teaching and revelation of both the natural and spiritual purpose for your face.

You will have also had an opportunity to be healed, changed, enlightened and blessed yourself, before doing this exercise which will make it have more meaning and purpose.

True relationship requires heart to heart openness, transparency and honesty. The face is an integral part of any true relationship. Often when relationships grow cold it is because the participants are no longer looking at one another or communicating face-to-face.

In many marriages that are having problems you will find that the couples no longer looks at each other in the eyes. They either communicate with their face turned away or hid in a newspaper or with a casual glance, but not really undivided attention, face-to-face.

Again, the eyes of the face reveal the emotions, which then reveals how someone is really feeling and also what they may actually need. When you are willing to look past the eyes of a person, with the objective of wanting to make the communication about them, you will see their soul, their emotions and the things that may not be obvious to the naked eye or the casual glance.

The purpose of this exercise is to allow you to practice speaking the Aaronic blessing face-to-face with another person. You do not have to know the person to do this exercise; in fact it may have an even more revelatory effect if you do not know them.

Face-to-Face Exercise Interaction:

1. Sit facing one another (two people at a time). You may do this more than once, but only two people should be facing each other at a time.

2. Turn to Numbers Chapter 6, verses 23-27. (Do not read them yet)

3. Holding each others hands, look into the eyes (soul) of the other person for 60 seconds. It is important to hold hands, as there is something about holding the hand that brings feelings of peace, comfort and safety.

   It causes you to be willing to allow someone else, to see your inner self as they look into your eyes. Give them permission to come into your intimate zone, by saying to them *"This is my God given face. Will you embrace who he has made me to be? If so, then I give you permission to come into my intimate zone, as I believe you will do me no harm."*

4. Do not talk or laugh even if you have the urge. Looking into someone's eyes without being intimidating is difficult and allowing someone to look into your eyes (soul), is even more difficult.

It is okay to smile but don't hide your inner emotions, by laughing it off.

Look into the person's eyes with the intent of seeing what they may need. Look not just to see, but to "hear" what their soul is saying. Look to see if they need encouragement, strength or assurance that someone cares for them, including God. Look into their eyes with a desire to see how you may be a joy and a comfort to them as you speak the Aaronic Blessing of the Lord over them.

Note:

Many people have been known to begin weeping when someone looks into their eyes with caring, versus anger or criticism. *If you begin to weep during this 60 seconds of gazing, it is okay, in fact, it is down right good!*

5. Choose which of you will speak the blessing first. Then, still holding hands and looking into their eyes, bless the person by speaking Numbers 6:24-26 over them. Speak directly to them, slowly, one verse at a time sincerely from your heart. Believe that you have the authority to do this.

Scripture teaches us to even bless those who curse us, so do not feel that you do not have the right to speak this blessing over someone (Matt. 5:44-45).

119

Once you have spoken verses 24 –26, personalize verse 27 by speaking it this way: ***"The blessing I have just spoken over you has invoked the Name of the Lord upon you and He will bless you. Do you receive this blessing?"*** Hopefully, their response will be "Yes."

6. Now, let the recipient of the blessing repeat this interaction with the other person. ***Again, do not start talking or laughing.***

7. When the blessing has been spoken over both of you, then each one should speak from their heart over one another, based on what looking in their eyes revealed to them. You may choose to say a prayer and/or blessing from your own heart. You may speak what you feel they need or what you desire to give from your heart. Sometimes the blessing you desire for yourself is good to pray for someone else, i.e., Shalom (love, peace, joy, wisdom, safety, health, prosperity).

Warning: This is not the time for flattery and speaking things that are not truth or from the Spirit of the Lord. God hates flattery, because it is of the flesh and its motive is deceitful and selfish.

---

8. Now receive the true revelation about ***your*** face. Allow yourself to be released from any shame that has to do with your physical appearance, your eyes, nose, lips, hair, ears, shape of head, cheeks, and/or chin.

9. Allow your emotions to be healed and released from the negatives things and words that have been imparted to you through the faces of others, including your own. Release any self-hatred you have built up, no matter who is to blame. Let

go of all guilt, shame, self-condemnation or bitterness.

10. Finally, accept your face as being created by God, for the purpose of being "the place of blessing" in the lives of others.

Note: Consider doing the Face-to-Face Interaction with your spouse, children, other relatives and friends. You will never be the same again. This interaction of speaking this blessing over others and receiving it for ourselves, opens the door to healing, forgiveness, reconciliation and restoration with man and with God Himself. The Bible states, "Pleasant words are as an honeycomb, sweet to the soul and healing to the bones." How much more are not the blessings that invoke the Name of the LORD!

May you be enriched, changed, enlarged and fulfilled as you begin to live a victorious face-to-face life and relationship with your Creator and others.

If you would like to contact A Taste of Jesus Ministries, for more information or for ministry engagements you may do so by email at **atoj100@sbcglobal. net** or write to:

DeLoris jacqueline Moore
A Taste of Jesus Ministries
P.O. Box 396
Flossmoor, IL 60422-0396